AROUND Orlando WITH KIDS

D0048768

by Jennie Hess

Fodor's Travel Publications
New York • Toronto • London • Sydney • Auckland

www.fodors.com

CREDITS
Writer: Jennie Hess

Series Editors: Karen Cure, Andrea Lehman
Editor: Melissa Klurman
Editorial Production: Linda K. Schmidt
Production/Manufacturing: Yexenia Markland

Design: Fabrizio La Rocca, *creative director;*
Tigist Getachew, *art director*
Illustration and Series Design: Rico Lins, Karen Ora,
Admoni/Rico Lins Studio

ABOUT THE WRITER

Jennie Hess is a travel and feature writer based in Orlando, Florida. A former newspaper journalist, Hess was a publicist for Walt Disney World Resort from 1988 through 1999. Today, she enjoys sharing the "inside scoop" on Orlando with visitors—including insights gleaned from her husband and two sons.

ISBN 0-679-00906-X
ISSN 1537-5528
First Edition

IMPORTANT TIP

Although all prices, opening times, and other details in this book are based on information supplied to us at press time, changes occur all the time in the travel world, and Fodor's cannot accept responsibility for facts that become outdated or for inadvertent errors or omissions. So always confirm information when it matters, especially if you're making a detour to visit a specific place.

SPECIAL SALES

Fodor's Travel Publications are available at special discounts for bulk purchases for sales promotions or premiums. Special editions, including personalized covers, excerpts of existing guides, and corporate imprints, can be created in large quantities for special needs. For more information, contact your local bookseller or Special Markets, Fodor's Travel Publications, 280 Park Avenue, New York, NY 10017. Inquiries from Canada should be directed to your local Canadian bookseller or sent to Random House of Canada, Ltd., Marketing Dept., 2775 Matheson Boulevard East, Mississauga, Ontario L4W 4P7. Inquiries from the United Kingdom should be sent to Fodor's Travel Publications, 20 Vauxhall Bridge Road, London, England SW1V 2SA.

PRINTED IN THE UNITED STATES OF AMERICA
10 9 8 7 6 5 4 3 2 1

CONTENTS

GET READY, GET SET!

Everyone knows that organizing a family's schedule is a full-time job. Pickups, drop-offs, school, parties, after-school activities—everyone off in their own direction. Of course, it's an organizer's dream, but a scheduling nightmare. Spending time together shouldn't be another thing to have to figure out.

We know what it's like to try to find great places to take your children or grandchildren. Sometimes it's tough to change plans when you suddenly hear about a kid-friendly event; besides, a lot of those events end up being crowded or, worse, sold out. It's also hard to remember places you read about in a newspaper or magazine, and sometimes just as hard to tell from the description what age group they're geared to. Who wants to bring a "grown-up" 12-year-old to an activity that's intended for his 6-year-old sister? Of course, if you're visiting Orlando, it's even harder to figure out the best things to do with your kids before you even get there. That's where we come in.

What you'll find in this book are 60 ways to have a terrific couple of hours or an entire day with your children or grandchildren, nieces or nephews. We've scoured the city and the surrounding area digging out activities your kids will love—from the myriad thrills of the area's famous theme parks to natural retreats that offer canoeing and wild Florida manatee sightings. The best part is that it's stress-free, uncomplicated, and easy for you. Open the book to any page and find a helpful description of a kid-friendly attraction, with age ratings to make sure it's right for your family, smart tips on visiting so that you can get the most out of your time there, and family-friendly eats nearby. The address, telephone number, open hours, and admission prices are all here for your convenience. We've done the work, so you don't have to.

Naturally you'll still want to keep an eye out for seasonal events that fit your family's interests, from the Annual Mount Dora and Winter Park art festivals in February and March to the Orlando International Fringe Festival—a 10-day downtown performance-arts street festival each spring. End-of-year holidays are done up big in the Orlando area, with festive celebrations at every theme park, including the Poinsettia Festival at Cypress Gardens. The Silver Spurs Rodeo, the Walt Disney World Marathon, baseball spring training season, and the PGA's Bay Hill Invitational bring athletes of all talents to the area all year. Spectacular fireworks displays erupt nightly over many area theme parks, and boating is a year-round pastime in this land of innumerable lakes. Farmers' markets sell fresh produce each weekend in downtown Orlando and Winter Park, and roadside stands overflow with seasonal goods ranging from tomatoes and strawberries to peaches and mangoes. In this popular vacation mecca where themed attractions rule, keep an eye out for the natural gems that make a visit special: Bald eagles and alligators in the wild, grandfather oaks dripping with Spanish moss, and sunsets that take your breath away.

WAYS TO SAVE MONEY

We list only regular adult, student (with ID), and kids' prices; children under the ages specified are free. It always pays to ask at the ticket booth whether any discounts are offered for a particular status or affiliation (but don't forget to bring your ID). Discounts are often available for senior citizens, AAA members, military personnel, and veterans, among others. Many attractions offer family memberships, generally good for one year of unlimited use for your family. These memberships sometimes allow you to bring a guest. Prices vary, but the memberships often pay for themselves if you visit the attraction several times a year. Sometimes there are other perks: newsletters or magazines, members-only previews, and discounts at a gift shop, for parking, or for birthday parties or special events. If you like a place when you visit, you can sometimes apply the value of your one-day admission to a membership if you do it before you leave.

Look for coupons—which can often save you $2–$3 per person—everywhere from the local newspaper to a shopping mall display to your pediatrician's office. In addition, sometimes groups of attractions get together and offer combination tickets, which are cheaper than paying for each one individually. One such bargain is the Orlando Flex ticket to Islands of Adventure, Universal Studios, Sea World, and Wet 'N Wild, good for any of 14 consecutive days at all four parks at a price lower than one-day admissions to all four parks ($159.95 plus tax ages 10 and up, $127.95 plus tax ages 3-9).

WHEN TO GO

Kid-oriented destinations are generally busiest when children are out of school—especially weekends, holidays, and summers. Saturday during the school year can be a good time to visit because tourists often travel on weekends and begin theme-park hopping Sunday or Monday. For outdoor attractions, it's good to visit during or after a rain, as crowds likely will have thinned out.

The hours we list are the basic hours, not necessarily those applicable on holidays. It's always best to check if you want to see an attraction on a holiday.

SAFETY

Obviously the amount of vigilance necessary will depend on the attraction and the ages of your kids. In crowded attractions, keep an eye on your children at all times, as their ages warrant. It's helpful to have kids wear bright, same-color T-shirts so they can be spotted easily if they stray. When you arrive, point out what the staff or security people are wearing, and find a very visible landmark to use as a meeting place, should you get separated. If you do split into groups, pick a time to meet. This will decrease waiting time, help you and your kids get the most out of your time there, and manage everyone's expectations.

FINAL THOUGHTS

Actually, this time it's yours, not ours. We'd love to hear what you or your kids thought about the attractions you visited. Or if you happened upon a place that you think warrants inclusion, by all means, send it along, so the next family can enjoy Orlando even more. You can e-mail us at editors@fodors.com (specify the name of the book on the subject line), or write to us at *Fodor's Around Orlando with Kids,* 280 Park Avenue, New York, NY 10017. We'll put your ideas to good use. In the meantime, have fun!

— THE EDITORS

ALL FIRED UP

There are few destinations where you can take the kids, grab a table, listen to upbeat music, and spend some fun creative time together. All Fired Up—a very kid-friendly paint-it-yourself pottery studio—is that kind of place. Owner Camille Marchese says painting pottery is "good for the soul," and you can't help but relax as you and the kids choose a once-fired earthenware mug or piggy bank, decide on paint colors, grab a brush, and let your art flow. When you first arrive, you can choose from at least 300 unfinished ceramic pieces including dog bowls, race-car banks, picture frames, plates, and cups. Most are functional items that make great gifts. After you and the kids get settled at a table, Marchese or one of her staff will show you how to create a design with stencils, stamps, or free-form drawing. You can pencil a design directly onto the piece if you want a guide to follow.

HEY, KIDS! Pottery art is ancient, and even now it begins with raw mud that's treated and fired before winding up as a "bisque" or ceramic mug or a bowl. After you've designed and painted your piece, the studio's staff adds a liquid glaze and returns it to a 1,836°F kiln to set the protective coating and finish it. Presto! If you made a mug, it's microwave safe. If you've created a bank, it will hold all your dough. And if you made Fido a dog bowl, he'll be a happy woofer.

364 W. Fairbanks Ave., Winter Park

407/644–9363;
www.allfireduponline.com

 $8 studio fee ages 13 and up before 7 PM, $10 after 7; $6 ages 12 and under

 Tu–Th 11–11, F–Sa 11 AM–12 AM, Su 1–7; closed most holidays

4 and up

Let the painting begin! After you've selected your paint from among 100 colors, you'll use a wide brush for large surfaces and a narrow brush for small designs, corners, and edges. Ask for guidance when deciding how many coats you'll need and which areas to paint first and last. While you work, have a latte or soft drink served in the studio. Or bring your own lunch or dinner and nosh while you work. Plan about two hours to complete your artwork. When you've finished, leave your pieces for All Fired Up staff to fire and glaze in their kilns. You can collect your pottery five to seven days later or have it shipped. Don't worry about the mess—All Fired Up does the dirty work.

KEEP IN MIND
The average price of pottery pieces is between $8 and $15, but paints, brushes, stencils, and other tools are included in your studio fee, as are the glazing and firing. The average per person cost is $16 to $20. Shipping costs depend on your pottery's size and weight.

EATS FOR KIDS Bring or order in food from **Bakely's Restaurant and Bake Shop** (345 W. Fairbanks Ave., tel. 407/645–5767), where meals include eggs and Belgian waffles served all day, as well as sandwiches, chicken finger baskets, and quesadillas. But if you'd prefer to drink a high-protein meal while you paint, order a heavenly Peanut Power smoothie from **Smoothie King** (360 W. Fairbanks, tel. 407/645–4509). Add a dash of chocolate or some strawberries for kick. There's a huge variety of smoothies, malts, and shakes on the menu, and children can get kids' kups of Choc-A-Laka, Gimme-Grape, and Berry Interesting.

AQUATIC WONDERS TOURS

59

Ask an experienced fisherman like Captain Ray what a child can learn from fishing, and he's quick to reel in an answer: how to be patient, how to handle minor disappointments, and how to "go with the ebb and flow." There's a lot more to fishing than the excitement of actually catching a fish, and Captain Ray of Aquatic Wonders gets a big kick out of helping families learn the ins and outs of this popular outdoor activity. Captain Ray captures kids' interest even before you board the boat. Up to six people at a time can head out with Ray on his 30' covered pontoon boat, *Eagle Ray,* for a half-day fishing adventure (four to five hours) on Lake Tohopekaliga, rated by *B.A.S.S.* magazine as one of Florida's top 10 lakes for bass fishing. Start out as early as possible (6 AM if you can handle it) and book ahead to avoid disappointment when you arrive at Big Toho Marina.

If you've never baited a hook, don't worry. Captain Ray will show you how with bread, worms, crickets, or wild shiners—small bait fish. He also knows all about the 32-odd

EATS FOR KIDS Pack up custom-made sandwiches, homemade soups, or the popular "Spiedies" sub at **Augie's Village Deli** (18 Broadway, tel. 407/846–8784). You can also get takeout PB&Js, ham and cheese, burgers, and other lunch standards at **Big Toho Marina** (101 Lakeshore Blvd., tel. 407/846–2124).

KEEP IN MIND Bring plenty of sunscreen, insect repellent, and a hat of some sort to shade your eyes. Captain Ray provides your rods, reel, and tackle if you don't have your own. Anyone 16 or older must purchase a Florida freshwater fishing license—you can get one at the Big Toho Marina bait shop. Beverages are available on the boat, but you can bring your own cooler full of drinks if you like. The Eagle Ray has a restroom on board and is accessible by wheelchair.

101 Lakeshore Blvd., Kissimmee

 $150–$200 boat charter for 2–6 passengers

 All hours

 407/846–2814;
www.florida-nature.com

 4 and up

species in the lake, including large-mouth bass, bluegill, crappie, speckled perch, and catfish that you just might hook on your expedition. Children who've never gone fishing usually can learn fast, and if they catch the "big one," Captain Ray will help them get a State of Florida certificate of commendation for their fishing finesse. While your family is trolling, you may also get lucky enough to see an eagle or other large bird swoop toward the lake for a fish (inevitably, they'll catch one a lot faster than you will). Chances are you'll also see alligators, otters, and some of the 135 species of birds that make the lake habitat their home. If the kids enjoy the boat experience, you may want to try Aquatic Wonders Tours' two-hour Eagle Watch Tour, a two-hour nighttime Gator Watch Tour, and other cruise adventures.

HEY, KIDS! You'll be singing, "Don't Worry, Be Happy" like Big Mouth Billy Bass if you catch a real largemouth bass in Lake Toho. In Florida, bass grow bigger than they do in northern lakes because of the warmer climate and longer growing season, so don't be surprised if you hook an 8–10 pounder. And don't be shocked if you pull in a catfish, complete with whiskers, or a gar, a bizarre, prehistoric-looking fish often measuring more than 2' with armor-plated scales and a long snout filled with teeth.

ARABIAN NIGHTS

58

Take a cast of 55 show horses, 30 stunt riders and other performers, a 90,000-square-foot dinner-theater arena, special-effects fog and snow, lively music, Moorish-themed sets, and a story filled with humor and drama, and you've discovered Arabian Nights—a unique dinner show with fairy-tale charm. Based on Walter Farley's best-selling *Black Stallion* book series, this long-running, oft-revised, 105-minute spectacle is big family entertainment at a reasonable cost.

Thirteen breeds of horses from around the world—including Arabians, Lippizzaners, and Appaloosas—are riveting as they prance, gallop, and strut through scenes that include Roman riding, bareback riding, chariot racing, trick riding, and even square dancing. Yes, these equestrian beauties can square dance—with a little guidance from their riders! A joking genie, resplendent in purple and gold, keeps young children laughing, and somehow it all works with the storyline of this romantic adventure. Girls love the hint of romance

KEEP IN MIND Though you can bring your 1-and 2-year-olds to the show for free, they probably will get restless, and you may miss some of the best acts of this intermission-free spectacle. Bring children who can sit through a full-length feature film. And don't rush out as soon as the show ends. Performers gather ring-side to sign autographs and pose for pictures, and children love getting an up-close look at the horses.

6225 W. Bronson Hwy.
(Hwy. 192 and I-4), Kissimmee

 $36.95 ages 12 and up,
$23.95 children 3–12

 Su–Th 7:30 PM, W–Sa 6 and 8:30 PM;
times may vary seasonally

407/396-7400, 800/553-6116,
800/533-3615 in Canada

 5 and up

and glittering costumes, boys eat up the adventure, and everyone cracks up during one scene of horse-and-cowboy slapstick.

You and your family munch on salad and rolls as the production opens on the wedding eve of fabled Princess Scheherazade of the literary Arabian Nights. Though her happiness is threatened by a Darth Vader–like character on horseback, the princess enjoys prenuptial festivities arranged by the genie. It's hard to focus on your food as the plot unfolds and you get caught up in the amazing horse-and-rider stunt work. One bareback rider leaps through a fire hoop and another skips rope atop her mount. Walter Farley's own Black Stallion puts in a memorable performance sans rider. The exciting ending can't help but put a smile on your face, so sit back, eat up, and enjoy!

EATS FOR KIDS

Arabian Nights' ticket price includes a three-course dinner, and the show's limited dinner menu is designed to satisfy most palates. You can choose from entrees of prime rib, vegetable lasagna, or chicken tenders. Salad, rolls, and a specialty dessert that's part of the plot also are served along with unlimited soft drinks, wine, beer, tea, and coffee.

HEY, KIDS! The smallest horse in the Arabian Nights show is called a Miniature Horse, and the largest is the Belgian. Can you pick them out from the ones in front of you? They're both featured in the gypsy act. The Miniature is 9 hands tall, and the Belgian is more than 19 hands tall. A hand is a measurement that equals 4"—horses are measured from hoof to shoulder blade. Don't forget to watch for the Black Stallion, and keep your eyes peeled for a magical four-legged creature!

AUDUBON'S CENTER FOR BIRDS OF PREY

57

Stevie-Ray is a bald eagle with a new lease on life. Blinded by exposure to pesticides, the endangered bird was scooped up by Florida Audubon's National Center for Birds of Prey and, believe it or not, fitted with custom contact lenses that restored his eyesight. The Maitland center has been key to rescuing eagles and other birds of prey such as hawks, owls, and falcons since 1979. And it has expanded its visitor-friendly wildlife rehabilitation center, where you can learn about the birds and the impact humans have on their environment. You and the kids will get a behind-the-scenes look into the medical exam lab where the center's staff works with the birds. Innovative medical breakthroughs including use of prosthetic beaks, laser surgery, and whirlpool bath therapy help rehabilitate the birds. You can also stroll a boardwalk by Lake Sybelia where birds in recovery do flight exercises. Walkways are interspersed with interactive exhibits, and graphics tell a self-guided conservation story highlighting the importance of birds of prey. This is a great place to connect with nature and to marvel at the majesty of these amazing creatures.

KEEP IN MIND You and the kids can play an active role to help save birds of prey. Visit www.adoptabird.org, where you can find photos and details about rescued birds and contribute to their care. A list of on-line merchants contributes a share of your purchase to the cause.

HEY, KIDS! Birds of prey hunt and feed on animals like mice, rabbits, fish, snakes and insects. They play a crucial role in the circle of life by feeding on small animals to keep them from overpopulating. Their eyesight is amazing—they can see small movements from two miles in the air. Their strong talons—sharp, curved claws—help them catch prey. Eagles and hawks are diurnal, or active by day, and that's when they hunt. Owls are nocturnal and usually hunt at night. Vultures are birds of prey, too, eating road kill and other dead animals and have been aptly dubbed "nature's flying garbagemen."

The center handles the largest volume of eagles, owls, falcons, hawks, and kites (predator birds with long, forked tails) east of the Mississippi River, averaging more than 650 admissions of injured or orphaned birds of prey each year. Several thousand birds, including more than 220 bald eagles, have been released back to the wild after receiving care here. You get an up-close look at the center's birds when you stroll along the Hawk Walk, the Owl Prowl, and the Eagle Aviary. Many of the birds' injuries prevent their release, and you'll see more than 21 species at the lakeside aviary where non-releasable birds reside.

When pioneers first formed the Audubon Society in the late 1800s, they committed to "save the wild birds." It's inspiring to see, more than a century later, how diligently the Center for Birds of Prey works to preserve that commitment.

EATS FOR KIDS Around the corner is a popular Italian deli where you can get great pizza, kids' pasta portions, and other Italian specialties— **Antonio's La Fiamma/Deli and Café** (611 S. Orlando Ave., Maitland, tel. 407/645–1039). **Bubbalou's Bodacious Bar-B-Q** (1471 Lee Rd., Winter Park, tel. 407/628–1212) is a tiny eatery with a big local following for its chicken, ribs, and other barbecue platters. For breakfast, lunch, or brunch, you can't beat **First Watch Restaurant** (1221 S. Orlando Ave., Maitland, tel. 407/ 740–7437) with its specialty pancakes, French toast, and creative egg concoctions.

BLUE SPRING STATE PARK

There's something about the endangered Florida manatee that evokes warm and fuzzy feelings despite the creature's wet, dirigible-like countenance. Once thought by sea-weary mariners to be some sort of mermaid, the docile manatee cruises the warm waters of Florida, munching vegetation and trying to avoid the deadly propellers of recreational boaters. When the waterways get cold—usually around November—a favorite manatee haunt is Blue Spring State Park, where the spring water bubbles up to an agreeable 72°F. Through early March, up to 150 manatees—also called sea cows—swim from the St. Johns River to gather at the spring. You'll be able to watch these unusual mammals swimming in the spring, often with babies by their sides. You may also get a chance to talk with state park ranger Wayne Hartley, a park veteran who names the manatees and documents their travels.

Make sure the kids keep watch for Millie, a real traveler who has been photographed virtually everywhere on the east coast of Florida in the past 15–20 years. At nearly 3,000 pounds,

HEY, KIDS! You can learn more about saving endangered manatees by checking out www.savethemanatee.org. You can even adopt a Florida manatee by sending a contribution to the Save the Manatee Club (tel. 800/432–JOIN). You'll get an adoption certificate and a photo and biography of "your" manatee. Fewer than 3,000 manatees exist today, and each year, injured and orphaned manatees require treatment from boat accidents. Some can be released right away, but others are cared for at Sea World Orlando and other locations until they're able to survive on their own.

she's also one of the biggest manatees sighted. Brutus and Merlin have been Blue Spring regulars since 1970 when Jacques Cousteau shot footage here. Another denizen, Howie, once inadvertently flipped Hartley's research canoe and destroyed the ranger's three cameras. Hartley enjoys pointing out his manatee friends for visitors. Sadly, he says it's easy to identify each manatee by the scar patterns left by boat propeller strikes. Hartley and the other park rangers run a Manatees of Blue Spring program in the park's concession building (1:30, 2:30, and 3:30 daily, with an extra 11 AM program weekends and holidays) with a film about the manatees and a question-and-answer session. Make a fall or winter day of it by packing a picnic, a volleyball (nets are available), and a pair of hiking shoes. Take it from the manatees, Blue Spring State Park is a terrific cool-weather retreat.

EATS FOR KIDS

What better way to celebrate a crisp Florida day than with burgers, hot dogs, and veggies on the grill? The park has charcoal grills and two large firepit grills available. Pull into one of Central Florida's myriad **Publix** or **Wynn Dixie** supermarkets for all the trimmings.

KEEP IN MIND When the weather gets warm, the manatees return to the St. Johns River and beyond. Once they're gone, you can swim in the spring (lifeguards are on duty from about Memorial Day through Labor Day). If your kids are mature enough, your family might enjoy a tour of the Thursby House (Th–Su, 11–4, 50¢ admission) adjacent to the stream. Settled by citrus growers, the house is restored to the period 1875–87 when steamboats plied the St. Johns as a main source of transportation.

BOGGY CREEK AIRBOAT RIDES

Millions of alligators populate the lakes, canals, and rivers of Florida, yet when was the last time you saw one in the wild? Climb aboard an airboat that tours vast Lake Tohopekaliga ("Toho" to the locals), and you'll likely see 8' and 9' alligators cruising blissfully past your 25' aluminum craft. Your boat, piloted by a U.S. Coast Guard captain and powered by an 8' propeller inside a giant "cage," skims the lake surface at speeds up to 38 mph for a true wind-in-your-hair experience. Boggy Creek captains provide ear protection for all riders, and they shut down the boat's loud engine frequently to point out wildlife along the way.

Kids love the excitement of these fast, noisy boats, and they can't help but soak up some facts during the memorable half-hour eco-experience. Go early or late if you can—before 10:30 AM, wildlife is most abundant; and late in the day there's a certain tranquility as a sinking sun glistens on the water's mirrorlike surface and the afternoon heat fades away.

HEY, KIDS!

Ask your captain to help you search for the legendary Godzilla—a 1,000-pound, 15' gator that hangs out in Friar's Cove, at about the halfway point of your Lake Toho ride.

EATS FOR KIDS A few miles up the road from the Boggy Creek Southport location in the Oak Bridge Commerce Park is a terrific family-run Italian eatery, **LeMay's Pizza** (tel. 407/870–2600 or 407/870–2700). Kids love the white pizza made with ricotta, mozzarella, and garlic butter. Subs, salads, pasta, and calzones also hit the spot. LeMay's will deliver your order before or after your boat tour so you can enjoy a picnic on the tables near the lake.

As your boat pushes through the grasses of these Florida Everglades headwaters, you'll pass unflinching blue herons and snowy egrets. Perky coots skitter across the water before taking flight. A sandhill crane guards her nest, and a young bald eagle soars above the pines at Toho's edge. You'll also see osprey, wood storks, turtles, and other native wildlife. Miles of cypress trees line the 23,000-acre lake, their knobby stumps protruding here and there.

Boggy Creek airboat tours also run from the East Lake Fish Camp in Kissimmee, and both locations offer the more adventurous night tours—great for older children. For an hour after the sun sets, you'll cruise the waterway in search of the lake's largest gators. Your captain wears a miner's cap, its light scanning the water's surface. You can't help but feel a thrill when you spot the glow of red eyes on the lake and watch these primeval creatures in their glory.

KEEP IN MIND The Central Florida sun can be brutal from late morning through the afternoon, so be sure to slather the kids with sunscreen before hopping aboard. Sunglasses are a big plus, too.

BOK TOWER GARDENS

Bok Tower Gardens may be one of Florida's most tranquil attractions, but it's full of curiosities to pique the interest of children. First, there's the novelty of climbing one of Florida's highest hills. In flat Florida, the gardens' location at almost 300' above sea level is akin to hiking a mountain. Near the hilltop is another novelty—the Bok "singing tower." This 5,500-ton marble and coquina Gothic tower rings daily with the music of an English carillon—an intriguing instrument of 57 bronze bells that weigh anywhere from 17 pounds to 12 tons each. Surrounding the tower are 200 acres of gardens, trails, and a live oak grove populated by 126 species of birds, a colony of wood ducks, squirrels, snakes, and other wildlife.

Begin at the visitor center, where kids can listen to prerecorded sounds of birds that live in the gardens. By the time they get outside, they'll know how to recognize the calls of

EATS FOR KIDS Inside the park, the **Carillon Café** offers counter-service, picnic-style lunches, including hot dogs. Turkey, ham, chicken salad, and other sandwiches are made to order and come with potato chips. **Lekarica Country Inn and Golf Course** (1650 S. Highland Park Dr., tel. 863/676–8281) is a family-owned eatery several miles from the gardens. It's open for Sunday brunch and lunch and dinner Tuesday through Saturday. Blueberry pork chops are popular, and although there's not a special menu for kids, the chefs will whip up kids' meals of burgers, grilled cheese, or other favorites if you ask for them.

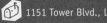 1151 Tower Blvd., Lake Wales

 $6 ages 13 and up,
$2 ages 5–12

 Daily 8–6; live carillon recital 3 PM,
recorded recitals throughout the day

 863/676–1408;
www.boktower.org

5 and up

mockingbirds, cardinals, and blue jays among many other birds. The center also houses the original carillon keyboard, called a clavier, so you can picture what's happening in the tower. The kids will want to measure their height against a cutout of the largest bell. Outside, one path leads to the window by a pond, where you can grab a wooden chair inside a rustic shelter and watch turtles, green herons, an alligator, and other pond creatures. Strolling toward the tower, you'll spot majestic white swans cruising past gigantic water lilies in the reflection pool beneath the tower. You might also see a harmless banded water snake or two slither out of the pool where fat golden koi swim close to the surface. When the bells ring out with songs such as "America the Beautiful" or Mozart's "Ring Bells, Ring," grab a park bench and let the kids frolic nearby, while you all enjoy the outdoor concert.

KEEP IN MIND
If you want to set up a picnic or toss a Frisbee, do it on the green area outside the garden's main entrance. Bring binoculars to make the tour more interesting for young garden and wildlife "detectives." Mosquitoes can be pesky in summer, so bring bug spray.

HEY, KIDS! Have your parents follow signs to Spook Hill just before you get to Bok Tower Gardens. Legend has it that, many moons ago, this former Native-American village was plagued by alligator attacks. A final battle between the chief and a vicious gator is said to have left the huge swampy depression nearby. Today, the ghost of the chief (or maybe the gator—no one is sure which) causes cars to roll uphill when you park your car in neutral at the white line painted on the road. Spook Hill is a right turn off Burns Avenue, then left and left again at Spook Hill Elementary School.

BUSCH GARDENS
FOR KIDS 7 AND UNDER

Busch Gardens rates high on the kid-friendly scale for the 7 and under crowd with its great mix of wild animal exhibits and pint-size children's rides. When you first arrive, walk through Myombe Reserve to watch the chimps and western lowland gorillas—they're usually most active before the heat of the day. Stroll through Edge of Africa where you can see hippos do their comical underwater dance and watch lions, meerkats, and other exotic creatures in habitats that mimic their natural homes. Stop by the elephant enclosure and animal nursery, both favorites of little ones, before hopping a ride at the Nairobi Train Station. The train circles the park's vast Serengeti Plain where you'll see giraffes, zebras, and antelopes. Youngsters love the thrill of the dark train tunnel just before the Congo Station, where you'll get off. Head straight for Timbuktu and a gaggle of great kiddie rides including teacups, planes, and motorcycles. If the kids are 6- or 7-year-old thrill seekers,

KEEP IN MIND In summer, long attraction waits can test the patience of even the most resolute. Try going off-season or when school's in session. And remember, with all the water attractions, it's smart to carry a backpack or tote with a change of clothes and towel.

EATS FOR KIDS There are places to dine or grab counter-service fare in nearly every "land" of Busch Gardens. On hot or rainy days, kids like to escape into **Das Festhaus** in Timbuktu, a 1,000-seat German festival hall where you can nosh on sandwiches, spaghetti, and other Italian dishes while watching costumed performers sing and dance. **Stanleyville Smokehouse** is a lure with its slow-smoked chicken and ribs. The small pizzas are winners at the **Provisions and Terrace** in Crown Colony. For full service, try the **Crown Colony House Restaurant's** seafood, sandwiches, and family-style dinners.

they'll want to try the Scorpion roller coaster (42" height requirement), the park's mildest coaster. Then backtrack to more kiddie rides across from Ubanga-Banga Bumper Cars in the Congo area before heading into Stanleyville. Here, kids 42" tall can ride the simplest flume, Stanley Falls.

Afterward, head south to Land of the Dragons. Kids will want to spend hours here climbing through the elevated maze of tunnels and rope bridges, splashing in a grotto of shallow water, and riding and "flying" in dragon-themed amusement rides. While the children have a blast, it's a good time for adults 21 and older to take turns visiting the nearby Hospitality House, where you can sample Anheuser-Busch–brand beers on the house.

HEY, KIDS! With 2,700 animals, Busch Gardens is one of the largest zoos anywhere. Its animals are well fed; in fact, each year the zoo kitchen uses 35,000 pounds each of carrots, apples, oranges, grapes, and bananas, and 87,600 pounds of Romaine lettuce and other greens as part of the critters' diets. But what goes in must come out, right? Here's the poop on how it's handled: each year, workers process 4 million pounds of animal waste at the park's own compost facility. The material is used to fertilize the park's lush landscaping, and park workers can take some home for their own gardens.

BUSCH GARDENS

FOR KIDS 8 AND UP

There's enough roller-coaster and flume action at Busch Gardens to keep kids 8 and older thrilled all day. First, though, steer your thrill-seekers over to Myombe Reserve and Edge of Africa to see the animals while they're frisky. If the line's not formidable, take the Rhino Rally safari from Nairobi to the Serengeti Plain. The 10-minute journey in an open Land Rover takes you close to endangered white rhinoceroses, Cape buffalo, warthogs, wildebeests, and other species and through an exhilarating flash-flood adventure. Then walk to Egypt to hit the inverted steel coaster Montu (54" height requirement). Actually, this coaster will hit you with nearly 4 Gs during your 3-minute flyby. Afterward, round the corner to Akbar's Adventure Tours (42" requirement) for a bumpy simulator ride before heading west to Gwazi, Florida's first double wooden roller coaster that swoops across a huge expanse of track. Take a stroll through Bird Gardens to catch your breath and stop at the Hospitality House for lunch or refreshments.

HEY, KIDS! Even though many of the wild animals at Busch Gardens appear to roam freely in their habitats, the 320 species of creatures that live here require a lot of special care. If you have Dr. Doolittle tendencies and are in sixth grade or up, you can check into several behind-the-scenes summer camps where you'll work with the animals alongside park zoologists and keepers. Campers help to prepare and deliver meals to the animals, and even help bathe some of them. Call 800/372–1797 or go to www.buschgardens.org. Plan to register early.

After your break, trek north to Stanleyville for a very quick spin on the Python (48" requirement) coaster and a very wet ride on the Tanganyika Tidal Wave (48" requirement). You may want to watch this one splash down before you commit to the ride's intense soaking. From here, it's a short walk to the Congo area of the park. Kumba (54" requirement) is another monster coaster favorite, and Congo River Rapids (48" requirement) is an excellent rafting adventure for the family. Stop by Claw Island to see some magnificent yellow and rare white Bengal tigers in a large habitat. Most kids can't resist the Ubanga-Banga Bumper Cars before heading down to Timbuktu. Try your luck at Sultan's Arcade and Games of Skill, where a pay-for-play win may yield a giant stuffed animal. The downside: you'll have to carry the fuzzy guy around for the rest of the day.

KEEP IN MIND From the Orlando area, it takes an hour or longer to drive here on I-4 west, then I-75 north to the Temple Terrace exit. Get an early start so you won't miss the animals when they're most fun to watch—in the earliest part of the day.

CANAVERAL NATIONAL SEASHORE

At the southern end of Canaveral National Seashore's 24 miles of pristine sand, dunes, and ocean sits Playalinda Beach, an undeveloped wonder of nature open for swimming and sunbathing. The fun of getting to this barrier island begins when you cross the Indian River intracoastal waterway to S.R. 402. Now you're in the Merritt Island National Wildlife Refuge, and to the south you'll see the space shuttle launch pads of NASA's John F. Kennedy Space Center. Stop at the refuge visitor information center, splash on some insect repellent, and stroll the center's boardwalk to see butterflies, turtles, and maybe even an alligator or two. Highlights include interactive wildlife exhibits that explain how sea turtles nest and how eagles and other animal species survive in the refuge. Grab some maps and brochures, pile back into the car, and continue along Rt. 402 to Playalinda. If the kids are interested, make one more stop to hike one of the refuge walking trails clearly marked on the way to the beach. More than 1,000 plant species and 310 bird species live in the area's hammock,

EATS FOR KIDS Plan a picnic on the beach. Stop at the **Subway** on S.R. 406 (2851 Garden St., tel. 321/264–2229) for subs, salads, and tortilla wraps. Kids' meals are only $2.64 and include one of the eatery's home-baked cookies and a soft drink.

KEEP IN MIND Lifeguards usually are on duty from Memorial Day through Labor Day, but always check the morning's information on strong rip currents and make sure you and the kids avoid them. If you see lightning, stay in your car until the storm passes completely. Restrooms, but not showers, are available in each small beach parking lot. You must bring your own food, water, and other beverages (no glass). The beach closes for three days prior to each shuttle launch, so check the schedule before making the excursion. Other activities available are horseback riding and camping.

East from Orlando on S.R. 528 or S.R. 50, N. on I-95 to S.R. 406, then 12 miles east of Titusville on S.R. 402

321/267-1110 beach, 321/861-0667 wildlife refuge; www.nps.gov/cana

$5 per vehicle

Year-round, 6 AM–8 PM during daylight saving hours; 6–6 standard time

All ages

lagoon, salt marsh, and pine flatland habitats. West Indian manatees, wood storks, and peregrine falcons are some of the endangered species residing here. If the kids are small and not up to hiking, plan a late afternoon or early evening drive over to the manatee observation area or a leisurely, self-guided drive along Black Point Wildlife Drive on your way home.

Playalinda Beach has been the site of local controversy for years because nude sunbathers also enjoy its unspoiled beauty. It's against the law to show up without a swimsuit, however, and you won't encounter anyone in the buff as long as you stay on the beach's southern half. So suit up, raise the beach umbrella, ride some waves with the kids, help them build a castle, and enjoy the beach as it was meant to be.

HEY, KIDS! Three species of sea turtles—loggerheads, leatherbacks, and green sea turtles—nest at Canaveral National Seashore from May through August. At night, the giant turtles emerge from the surf and lay up to 100 leathery eggs in each nest. Park rangers and volunteers screen the nests to prevent destruction by raccoons. Hatchlings then pass through the mesh openings at night to scramble back to sea for survival. Park officials estimate more than 80 percent of turtle nests have been protected by the screening.

CENTRAL FLORIDA ZOO

It's rare to have an opportunity anywhere in the world to look an endangered cheetah in the eye or admire the markings on its coat up close. However, at the Central Florida Zoological Park, there's a little-known viewing spot at the cheetah habitat that gives you a peek at the fastest land animal on Earth (up to 70 mph). After you pass the llama and rhea (big bird) habitat, you'll see the cheetah cage. If the park's two males aren't nearby, turn the corner and walk the worn jungle pathway that borders the cage. The cheetahs often sit near the back, gazing out at visitors who find them. Check out the black striped markings by their eyes—they provide sun protection. Stay quiet, and you should get an excellent view.

This 88-acre zoo, with its well-marked exhibits, is a kid-friendly critter experience 20 miles north of downtown Orlando. Its animal population is diverse (more than 100 species), and it takes only a few hours to see. At the Animal Adventure Children's Zoo area, youngsters can feed a llama and pet goats and cows. Another kid favorite is the air-conditioned

HEY, KIDS! Keep an eye on the endangered Grand Cayman rock iguana, among the rarest lizards in the world. If it shakes its head, it's saying, "Keep out! This is my territory." The endangered Siamang, a type of ape, is also territorial and has been dubbed the "loudest land mammal" for its high-pitched hoots that can be heard far into the jungles of Southeast Asia (and around the zoo!). The name hippopotamus is Greek for "river horse," and it's another creature that guards its territory. Weighing up to 6,000 pounds, hippos have killed more humans than most African animals.

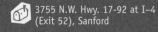

herpetarium. Here, a pane of glass separates you from Central Florida's four venomous snakes (the eastern diamondback rattlesnake, the water moccasin, the pygmy rattlesnake, and the colorful coral snake), as well as the fascinating horned rhinoceros viper of Africa and many other reptiles. As you navigate the park's boardwalks and mulched walkways, you'll see endangered hyacinth macaws, Asian elephants, and New Guinea crocodile monitors—the longest lizards in the world, measuring up to 13'. You can also watch primates and a variety of cats that include leopards, cougars, and the smallest species of wildcat in the world weighing between three and seven pounds—the Black-footed cat of southern Africa.

Many of the park's species are endangered, so it's nice to know that the zoo participates in the Species Survival Plan programs of the American Zoo and Aquarium Association to aid in wildlife conservation.

KEEP IN MIND
The zoo is always a better experience in fall, winter, or spring, when temperatures are more moderate. If possible, start out in the morning when the animals are friskier and avoid visiting when temperatures are expected to top 85 degrees.

EATS FOR KIDS In cool weather, pack a light picnic or have burgers, veggie burgers, or hot dogs at an outdoor table next to the park's snack bar—also be prepared to spring for a tasty, home-style root beer or cherry snow cone ($1.50) on your way out. At nearby Seminole Towne Center mall, you can have your pick of **Red Lobster** (20 Towne Center Circle, tel. 407/320–0888), **Steak 'n' Shake** (40 Towne Center Circle, tel. 407/328–8300), and several other popular chain eateries.

CIRQUE DU SOLEIL

In the world according to Cirque du Soleil (sirk-doo-solay), anything is possible. A cyclist rides upside down on a wire. A man flies. A cleaning lady kisses a frog and discovers she's met her prince. In the surreal world of "La Nouba"—a live show created just for its Downtown Disney theater—everyday life transforms into a series of astonishing, quirky, funny, and just-plain-thrilling moments. More than 70 performers from around the world, including gymnasts, dancers, high-wire and trapeze artists, weave the intriguing tale of "La Nouba," from the French phrase *"faire la nouba,"* which means "to party, to live it up." Live music, precision choreography, dazzling costumes, and dramatic sets are the finishing touches that make this fast-paced show truly one-of-a-kind—and definitely worth the somewhat high price of admission.

Children who can sit still and enjoy a full-length feature film generally adore a Cirque du Soleil performance. Between awesome acts by adolescent Chinese yo-yo performers, aerial

KEEP IN MIND If your children aren't used to staying up late, plan for a light early dinner when the restaurants aren't crowded, then hit the 6 PM show. Take a restroom break just before show time—there's no intermission, and you won't want to miss an act.

EATS FOR KIDS Before or after your show, stop by **Wolfgang Puck Cafe** (tel. 407/938–9653) several paces away. Puck pizzas and other goodies are kid favorites; sushi, pumpkin ravioli, and a menu full of innovative eats by the famous chef win adult raves. Prices are a bit high in the café, so if you're on a budget, grab pizzas, salads, and sandwiches at the restaurant's **Wolfgang Puck Express** counter and dine on the verandah. Also at Downtown Disney's West Side, **Bongos Café** (tel. 407/828–0999) offers Cuban fare and **House of Blues** (tel. 407/939–2648) has a mixed American menu including creole and Southern taste treats.

 Downtown Disney West Side

 $67 ages 10 and up, $39 ages 3–9

407/939–7600

  Shows Th–M 6 and 9 PM

5 and up

ballet artists, and high-wire walkers, two wacky clowns tickle your funny bone. Identical twin brothers perform gravity-defying acrobatics on a 6½' metal wheel, and a Russian balance artist builds a chair stack so precarious that you won't believe his feat at the top. So much happens so smoothly in 90 minutes that the standing ovation may take you by surprise.

When you see "La Nouba," be prepared to unleash your imagination. Interpret the show as you would an abstract art piece. Have fun talking about it with the kids. And don't be surprised if a few Cirque characters revisit you one night in your dreams.

HEY, KIDS: If you think your neighbor can do some fancy bike tricks, you haven't seen anything yet. Watch the BMX wizard's fancy footwork as he shows off his G-turns, boomerangs, and megaspins. And check out the muscle power of the second cycle performer as he hops the theater stairs on one wheel. Enjoy the awesome stunts, but don't try this at home!

CYPRESS GARDENS

More than 65 years ago, before theme parks sprouted all over Orlando, Cypress Gardens was a tourism king. The park's water ski stunt shows and lush gardens were world famous, and while today they remain a big draw, Cypress Gardens has planted a new lure for families with children—the Wacky Water Park. However, this kid-friendly area should be presented to children like a Popsicle after the main course. As you enter the park, first veer right to visit the park's Botanical Gardens. Keep an eye out for butterflies, blue herons, and other wildlife as you stroll past a cypress swamp, through a quaint "Victorian Garden Party" topiary, and into the serene Oriental Gardens. Next, head to the Ski Stadium to catch a show. Talented male and female water-skiers twist, turn, flip, and race in breathtaking stunts choreographed to a lively soundtrack. The show's veteran star, Corky the Clown, pops up several times with ski antics especially geared toward children.

Grab some lunch after the show, then head straight to Island in the Sky, a revolving, open-air tower that hydraulically lifts you 16 stories above the park for a great view. About 50

HEY, KIDS! You can learn about some interesting critters at the "Calling All Animals" show. A pair of blue and gold macaws may look sophisticated, but they'll always have the emotions and intelligence of 2-year-olds, according to the park's animal keepers. Hootie, the great horned owl, can swivel his head up to 270 degrees thanks to 14 vertebrae in his neck (humans have seven). Also here are North American possum. These critters are marsupials, and the babies are born after just 13 days of development, then climb into the mama possum's pouch. One hundred days after birth, they're on their own.

2641 S. Lake Summit Dr., Winter Haven, off U.S. 27, 22 miles south of I-4

 $34.95 ages 13 and up, $19.95 ages 6-12

 Daily 9:30-5; longer hours seasonally

800/282-2123, 863/324-2111; www.cypressgardens.com

 1 and up

paces from the sky tower is the entrance to Wacky Water Park via Carousel Cove. In the cove you'll find lots of kiddie rides, including planes and boats, geared toward the 5-and-under set. Just beyond the rides, it gets very wet beginning at the shallow Spunky's Lagoon, enhanced with spouting dolphins, a spraying elephant, and plastic palms. Beyond this kiddie pool, children (and adults) 3' and taller can soak up the fun on six Flumarama body slides—all tame enough for a 6-year-old to go it alone. After drying off, don't miss one of the park's "Calling All Animals" shows, or stroll through Cypress Junction's elaborate model railroad—two great ways to cap the afternoon.

KEEP IN MIND

Central Florida's daily summer thunderstorms often arrive late afternoon, but watch weather reports for an aberration so the kids don't miss the Wacky Water Park. Allow at least an hour or more for water play time. You'll find lockers and changing rooms just inside Carousel Cove.

EATS FOR KIDS Chow down on seafood or chicken salad while kids have a chicken-nugget basket at the park's **Crossroads Restaurant & Terrace** if you want full service. Close by is the **Village Fare Food Court,** with plenty of options including burgers, hot dogs, salads, and desserts. There's a dinner cruise on the park's **Southern Breeze** paddle-wheel boat (tel. 863/324-2111 ext. 445). On your way out of the park, you'll find tasty, inexpensive barbecue including the "Family Picnic" of chicken, pork, beef, ribs, turkey, baked beans, corn-on-the-cob, fries, and garlic bread at **Schack's** (3000 Cypress Gardens Rd., tel. 863/324-1537).

DELEON SPRINGS STATE PARK

You can't make reservations at the Old Spanish Sugar Mill Grill & Griddle House, but you shouldn't visit DeLeon Springs State Park without sampling the flapjacks within. This 1830s sugar mill, now a gristmill and down-home restaurant, is an experience worth the sometimes hours-long wait. Several paces from the cool waters of DeLeon Springs, the Sugar Mill grinds its own grain to concoct the pancake batter you cook yourself on griddles built into each table. Kids can't resist creating their own flapjacks with chocolate chips, sliced bananas, blueberries, or homemade peanut butter. For $4 apiece you'll get all you can cook and eat of both "Early American" unbleached white flour cakes and the five-grain cakes served with maple syrup, raw honey, and molasses.

To make room for the feast, explore some of this 603-acre state recreation area. Take a swim in the 72°F springs where lifeguards are on duty from early April through mid-August.

KEEP IN MIND The Sugar Mill is usually packed on holidays and summer weekends, so check in at the counter as soon as you arrive to put your name on the waiting list. You'll be called on a loudspeaker that can be heard anywhere near the springs.

EATS FOR KIDS Be creative when designing your pancakes—you can make dinosaurs, smiley faces, and other culinary works of art by arranging apple or banana slices, pecans, and other morsels on your batter. Each family-size dish of add-ons is $1, so you can get "the works" for just $7. (Chocolate lovers should go for two dishes of the chocolate chips). Coffee, smoothies, juices, and herb tea complement the cakes. You can add crispy bacon, ham, and even vegetarian sausage to your order for $1 each. Fruits and cheeses, sandwiches, and salads round out the menu.

A generous lawn shaded by giant live oaks surrounds the swimming hole, and you can plunk down beach towels and chairs before taking a dip. Or you can head out onto the springs run in a rental canoe to explore several acres of the Lake Woodruff National Wildlife Refuge. Paddleboats, inner tubes, and swim fins are available, too. If you want to go bass and bream fishing, anyone 16 and older will need a Florida freshwater fishing license. A half-mile nature trail that winds through a floodplain forest is a fun diversion for explorers. Don't miss checking out the remains of the original sugar mill on former plantation property just behind the restaurant. Originally built in 1831 by Col. Orlando Rees, the mill and plantation were destroyed several years later during the second Seminole War. The sugar mill was rebuilt during the 1840s and later converted to grind corn. The huge mill wheel, renovated and reattached to the mill—for authenticity, not function—was turned by the flow of spring water.

HEY, KIDS! Back in the mid-19th century, huge stalks of sugar cane were grown right next to the mill. Powered by the flowing springs, the mill wheel turned rollers that crushed the cane stalks to release their juices. The cane juice was boiled in kettles until the water evaporated and the sugar crystallized. Today, the Schwarze family—sixth-generation gristmillers—own the mill and crank up their French buhr millstones (via electricity) each night to grind corn, wheat, rye, buckwheat, and rice for their pancake batter and home-baked bread.

DISCOVERY COVE

The exhilaration leaves you breathless as you hitch a swift thrill ride on a powerful dolphin's dorsal fin, zipping through the chilly waters of Discovery Cove's Dolphin Lagoon. For animal lovers, this water park is the ultimate interactive experience. You'll be among a maximum of 1,000 guests admitted each day, so the only line you're likely to encounter is the one for the free buffet lunch. All you need is a swimsuit. Admission includes beach umbrellas, lounge chairs, towels, lockers, snorkel gear—even regulation sunscreen. In winter, wetsuits are complimentary. When you arrive, a friendly guide meets you at the welcome center and answers questions as you stroll the nature walk to the white-sand beach. Park your gear, then head for the water—anywhere except the Dolphin Lagoon, which is off limits until your scheduled swim time.

You can snorkel with reef fish and sharks at the Coral Reef (no worry—the sharks are separated from swimmers by an acrylic shield), or swim in the Ray Lagoon with dozens of stingrays, some up to 4' in diameter. Next, take a leisurely float in an inner tube along the Tropical

HEY, KIDS! You'll be swimming with Atlantic bottlenose dolphins, which average 8'–10' and weigh 300–600 pounds. Dolphins are extremely social, and communicate with squeaking, grunting, and trilling sounds. They send messages through body language by leaping out of the water and landing on their sides, or by smacking their tail flukes against the water. When you snorkel with the stingrays, if you hold out a hand, they'll take your finger in their mouths—don't worry though, it won't hurt because they don't have teeth.

River and through the Aviary, where you can hop off to study some of the hundreds of birds that make their home here. Leave some time for the beach and for playing in the large lagoon-like pool with waterfalls.

When it's your turn to swim with the dolphins (you're assigned a session between early morning and late afternoon), you'll begin with a 15-minute orientation in a beachside hut. You'll be in the water about 30 minutes total, possibly with another family (up to seven guests total), plus two dolphins and two trainers. After meeting the dolphins in Dolphin Lagoon's shallow waters, your group heads to deeper water for a swim alongside a dolphin or a swift ride holding on to the dolphin's dorsal fin. Cameras aren't allowed, but Discovery Cove photographers are busy snapping photos—for sale, of course, as you exit the water.

KEEP IN MIND
You don't need to be an exceptional swimmer to have fun here, but you should be able to float with the aid of a flotation vest. Plan to take advantage of a major perk: admission price includes a pass for seven consecutive days' admission to SeaWorld Orlando.

EATS FOR KIDS Don't bother bringing food in—it's not allowed. The buffet lunch is included in admission and includes kid favorites like fajitas, hot dogs, hamburgers, and desserts such as cakes, cookies, and chocolate pudding. Soft drinks, beer, pretzels, nachos, fresh fruit, and ice cream are for sale throughout the park. When you make your reservation, note if anyone in your group has a food allergy or special dietary needs. They'll then be able to select from a special lunch menu at check-in.

DISNEY-MGM STUDIOS
FOR KIDS 7 AND UNDER

There's a "Bear in the Big Blue House" at Disney-MGM Studios, and that's just one of many reasons why this theme park tickles youngsters 7 and under. Disney-MGM Studios is full of live shows and attractions built on the success of popular Disney television series or feature films. With Playhouse Disney (where Bear lives), *Beauty and the Beast*—Live on Stage, Voyage of *The Little Mermaid,* and The Magic of Disney Animation, you already have enough on the itinerary to fill half the day. Little ones love seeing these famous TV and film characters come to life on stage or on the tablets and computer screens of Disney animators who draw them for the movies. Check show schedules when you enter to optimize your time. Some attractions, like Mermaid, run continually, and Playhouse Disney and others are scheduled several times daily.

HEY, KIDS!

Several famous Disney villains try to defeat Mickey Mouse in the Fantasmic! evening spectacular. Name the films in which these villains first appeared: 1) Ursula, 2) Jafar, 3) Maleficent, and 4) Hades. Answers: 1. The Little Mermaid, 2. Aladdin, 3. Sleeping Beauty, and 4. Hercules.

KEEP IN MIND The Fantasmic! extravaganza fills its 6,900 seats early since seating begins two hours before showtime. Plan to tote some diversions and check in at least an hour ahead for decent seats. A tip: if you make dinner reservations at the park's Guest Services counter in the morning for the Hollywood & Vine buffet, Mama Melrose's Ristorante Italiano, or The Hollywood Brown Derby, you get VIP seating for the show minus the long wait. Be sure to request a splash-free zone.

When you're not taking in a show, hop a tram for the Studios Backlot Tour with its exciting (but not-too-terrifying) pass through Catastrophe Canyon. Explain to your kids ahead of time that it's all special effects, and that your tram is in no real danger. Before or after the tour, let children explore the *Honey, I Shrunk the Kids* playground while you watch. They can climb aboard a huge ant, tunnel beneath giant grass blades, scramble up a rope web, and slide down a strip of Kodak film. Nearby, Kermit and his Muppet pals are a hoot in Jim Henson's MuppetVision 3-D, where special effects and other surprises create more of a "4-D" experience. Don't miss The Magic of Disney Animation, where you can peek behind the scenes as artists work on upcoming Disney films. Here, you'll also see clips of famous Disney works in an attraction bursting with happy endings.

EATS FOR KIDS Fast-food kid favorites are the pizza at **Toy Story Pizza Planet Arcade** and hot dogs and burgers at the **Backlot Express.** Most kids also enjoy zooming on over to the **Sci-Fi Dine-In Theater Restaurant** (tel. 407/WDW–DINE) to chow down on sandwiches, pastas, and salads while sitting at tables in shiny vintage convertibles and watching hilarious old film trailers. Or let "mom" and "cousin Bertha" serve up meat loaf or chicken and a mean milk shake at the **50's Prime Time Café** as you tune into "I Love Lucy" and other '50s favorites on black-and-white TVs.

The lights and camera are draws, but kids 8 and up will go for the action at Disney-MGM's thrill attractions. First stop, the Rock 'n' Roller Coaster starring Aerosmith (for kids 48" or taller). With its twists, turns, and inversions bolstered by a loud rock sound track, this coaster draws big lines and may warrant a FASTPASS appointment (Disney's method of helping you avoid tiresome queues). Then head next door to get in line for The Twilight Zone Tower of Terror (40" height requirement). Rod Serling has a cameo in this stomach-flipping attraction culminating in a 13-story runaway elevator ride. Next stop, the Star Tours flight simulator where R2D2 and C-3PO accompany you on a high-speed space junket gone awry. Prepare for plenty of turbulence, although this is a tamer ride than the others you've visited so far. Synchronize your watches to catch a performance of the Indiana Jones Epic Stunt Spectacular, where explosions, fire, simulated gunfire, and an out-of-control aircraft ratchet up the excitement as stunt performers show how it's done in the movies.

HEY, KIDS! At Rock 'N' Roller Coaster, keep an eye out for "Hidden Mickeys" as you wait to ride. Imagineers, Disney's creative team, often design the famous mouse's mug into park attractions. Here, watch for the Big Cheese in the lobby's floor tile and on a poster of the "8th Street Kidz Band," where rocker "Jesse Camp" sports a denim jacket with a Mickey Mouse patch. At The Twilight Zone Tower of Terror, a little girl in the eerie story clutches a Mickey Mouse doll. Mickey's famous silhouette also appears as a water stain on the boiler room wall.

 Lake Buena Vista off I-4

$48 ages 10 and up, $38 ages 3–9; parking $6

407/824-4321;
www.disneyworld.com

 9–7; hours vary in summer and on holidays

3 and up

The Great Movie Ride is laid-back, but the whole family can ride these slow cars together. You'll see movie scenes starring Disney's Audio-Animatronics (robotic) film star re-creations, including Sigourney Weaver and some creepy visitors in *Alien* and the Wicked Witch in *The Wizard of Oz*. Around the corner and across Mickey Avenue, older kids with fast fingers might wind up in the hot seat on "Who Wants to Be a Millionaire—Play It!" The game-show knockoff hands out prizes instead of cash. The Backstage Pass attraction next door showcases special effects from *Pearl Harbor* the movie. A "lucky" visitor gets plucked from the audience and doused in a water effects scene as "missiles" and "bombs" explode nearby. Cap off your visit with more water effects, plus music, lasers, and fireworks at Fantasmic!, where the villains of Disney's world take on Sorcerer Mickey in a showdown of epic proportion.

KEEP IN MIND Walt Disney, who would have been 100 years old in 2001, became a cultural icon thanks to a little animated mouse named Mickey. The Magic of Disney Animation attraction, a working animation studio where new characters are born and film animation flourishes, is a tribute to his creative genius. Don't miss this opportunity to help kids discover what goes into all those classic cartoons they love so much and to appreciate the actual art of animation. Even though computers have created a brave new world of animation filmmaking, artists' meticulous hand drawings remain at the heart of Disney's beloved classics.

DISNEYQUEST

You're on the deck of a pirate ship firing a cannon as you navigate rough seas teeming with buccaneers. You aim your cannon and blast away to capture pirate treasure before facing the ultimate showdown with Jolly Roger and his ghost ship. It's time to defend your gold (and the rest of the family had better help!), because this is Pirates of the Caribbean: Battle for Buccaneer Gold, a 3-D, surround-screen, motion-based adventure that places your crew on the bow of a ship and in the middle of the action.

After you arrive at DisneyQuest—an indoor, interactive theme park—head straight for Pirates (first floor) or to CyberSpace Mountain (second floor). Here, you'll create a virtual roller coaster on a computer touch screen. You can then ride your creation in a motion simulator—guaranteed to make you scream if you've added lots of 360-degree maneuvers. Then move onto the first-floor's Virtual Jungle Cruise and its giant undulating rafts that you "paddle" down waterfalls, through molten lava, and past a pesky T-rex. Back on the second floor,

HEY, KIDS!
You can build a coaster at CyberSpace Mountain that's just your speed. After you've added all the loops and barrel rolls you can stand, the computer will rate your ride from 0 through 5. If it looks too scary (5), you can ratchet down to a 3 or 4 before you board.

KEEP IN MIND
Rainy days usually mean long lines here, so arrive at 10:30 AM on a sunny day, if possible. Kids must be 51" to ride CyberSpace Mountain or Buzz Lightyear's AstroBlaster and 35" to join the family in Pirates of the Caribbean. There's plenty of diversion nearby for younger kids, who really go for the row of free-play retro arcade games—Pac Man, Moon Patrol, Robotron—next to AstroBlaster. Strollers aren't allowed here, so don't bring infants or toddlers. Do bring a sweatshirt, however, because the building temperature can be very chilly.

Downtown Disney West Side
at Lake Buena Vista

 $29 ages 10 and up,
$23 ages 3–9

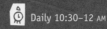 Daily 10:30–12 AM

407/824-4321;
www.disneyworld.com

5 and up

it's worth donning the bulky headset to embark on Aladdin's Magic Carpet Ride, a fast-paced virtual flying adventure through brilliantly animated scenes from Disney's *Aladdin*. And it's worth waiting for the interactive computer stations such as Magic Mirror (redesign and morph your face) and Radio Disney SongMaker (customize your theme song, then rock to the playback). The elementary set is especially happy here. At Buzz Lightyear's AstroBlaster bumper cars (third floor), you can shoot balls at other cars to make them spin. And the Mighty Ducks Pinball Slam is a blast if kids are heavy enough (about 75 pounds) or strong enough to control the "human pinball" life-size joystick platform. On the fourth floor, steer clear of the prize play games at MidWay on the Moon if you want to save your bucks. Complete your quest on Floor 5, where you battle comic book villains in the virtual Ride the Comix experience, then rescue the good guys and quash the bad in Invasion! An Extraterrorestrial Alien Encounter simulator.

EATS FOR KIDS You won't have to leave the building for lunch or dinner. **The Cheesecake Factory Express "FoodQuest"** on Floor 5 comes fully loaded with pizza, pasta, burgers, dogs, wraps, soups, and salads. Desserts at Floor 4's **Wonderland Café** (including several amazing cheesecakes) should be shared to avoid massive sugar overload. If you crave a change of ambiance after three or four hours inside, walk a few steps and grab a balcony seat at **Bongo's Cuban Café** (tel. 407/828-0999) for authentic, if not the finest, Cuban cuisine.

DISNEY'S ANIMAL KINGDOM
FOR KIDS 7 AND UNDER

44

If you're heading to Disney's Animal Kingdom with kids under 4, think again. Although animals are presented in an extraordinary fashion here, small children will get restless without the diversion of an occasional kiddie ride. The 4–7 crowd, however, will delight in Disney's menagerie of extinct, exotic, and endangered species. This isn't really a zoo, it's a theme park that promotes wildlife conservation. It's also a clever mix of shows, with interactive animal exhibits, an African-style safari, and a couple of thrill rides tossed in. Check the guidemap for show times as soon as you enter. Young children will want to see *Festival of the Lion King* and *Pocahontas and Her Forest Friends,* both running throughout the day in the themed land of Camp Minnie-Mickey. Here, kids can also pose for photos and get autographs of Mickey, Minnie, Goofy, Pluto, and the gang. And though animal cartoon characters usually reign with kids at Disney, the real animals are the attention grabbers on the Kilimanjaro Safaris, a ride in an open jeep across a 100-acre savanna. Hippos, elephants, lions, rhinos, antelope, cheetahs, and many other species roam the savanna in cleverly

EATS FOR KIDS Most kids' favorite lunch spot is **Restaurantosaurus** in Dinoland (tel. 407/WDW–DINE). You'll get counter-service burgers, salads, and even a McDonald's Happy Meal, unless you reserve priority seating for "Donald's Prehistoric Breakfastosaurus," complete with Disney character greetings. **Tusker House Restaurant** in Africa offers more quick-service variety, including the best cinnamon buns around and chicken with African spices. **Rainforest Café** (tel. 407/WDW–DINE) at the park's entrance is a wild way to end the day with great pastas, salads, ribs, and dinosaur-shaped chicken tenders for the kids.

secured habitats that give you a sense of intruding on free-roaming animals. A typically Disney safari storyline involving animal poaching may seem contrived to adults, but kids eat it up.

The Boneyard at Dinoland U.S.A. is Disney's best interactive play area. Kids can spend hours exploring this "dig site" complete with multiple climbers and slides built into "rocks." They can even dig into a huge sandbox to uncover mammoth bones. Afterward, trek back to Discovery Island and "It's Tough to Be a Bug" inside the Tree of Life. The 3-D, special effects cartoon-based show is a hoot for kids (as long as they're not afraid of the dark and noisy surprises) and adults. If you're here for a full day, don't miss the train to Rafiki's Planet Watch, where a petting yard, animal demonstrations, and easy-to-use computers make conservation fun for everyone.

KEEP IN MIND
Easy-to-read bird-spotting guides are available on loan in the park's two aviaries. Use them to help spot and identify the colorful species flitting between the branches.

HEY, KIDS! If you're feeling kind of buggy after seeing "It's Tough to Be a Bug," there's good reason. There are more than 1 million animal species known to science, and 750,000 of those species are insects. Though humans don't give them much respect, we can't ignore bugs' contributions to entertainment over the years. Consider Jiminy Cricket, Charlotte and her web, The Fly, and Flight of the Bumblebee. Years ago, legions of hard-working ants were stars of the feature film *Antz* with Woody Allen, and also Disney's *A Bug's Life,* from which "It's Tough to Be a Bug" was derived.

If the kids are over 8, your adventure should begin at Kilimanjaro Safaris first thing in the morning. If the wait is longer than 30 minutes, grab a FASTPASS appointment (Disney's answer to avoiding long lines) and take the Pangani Forest Exploration Trail next door. Morning is the best time to see most of the animals because they're more active before temperatures rise, and you might catch the gorillas cavorting in their lush habitat. Ride the safari, then head to Asia for a Kali River Rapids FASTPASS. Hit the Maharajah Jungle Trek while you wait. Fruit bats, tigers, a Komodo dragon, and other critters are fascinating to watch in habitats almost identical to their natural homes. When you board a raft for the white-water rapids of Kali River, prepare for a plunge factor that guarantees wet clothing. Dry off on your way to DinoLand U.S.A., where you can pick up a DINOSAUR thrill ride FASTPASS. Then have lunch at Restaurantosaurus before your DINOSAUR adventure. Let your lunch settle before you board. This wild ride, mostly in the dark, shakes you up on a twisting

HEY, KIDS! Trees and plants play a big role in this park. But how did Disney get Orlando to look like the jungles of Africa? Just some of the supporting players: the enormous Tree of Life looks so natural due its 103,000 fabric leaves with five different shades of green, blowing in the wind. The towering acacia trees, like those seen on a real African safari, actually are 30' Southern live oaks with a close-cropped crew cut. Leafless baobab trees on the savanna may look like the real thing, but they're sculpted with wire and cement!

Lake Buena Vista off I-4

 407/824-4321;
www.disneyworld.com

 $48 ages 10 and up, $38
ages 3-9; parking $6

8-6; hours vary in summer
and on holidays

4 and up

journey back in time as you dodge prehistoric monsters and earth-shattering asteroids. Kids tall enough to ride (40") usually want to do it again.

While in DinoLand, catch a performance of Tarzan Rocks! The action rarely wanes during this 30-minute live show of extreme skating, gymnastics, and rock music. At this point, 8- to 12-year-olds will want to join the younger set for some Boneyard antics. Then head back to the park's Discovery Island hub. Unless the wait is longer than 45 minutes, skip your FASTPASS option for the Tree of Life's "It's Tough to Be a Bug" show. The queue meanders along paths surrounding the tree, and you and the kids can search for the 325 different animals carved into its monstrous Disney-engineered trunk. You'll also have a chance to spot Discovery Island kangaroos, lemurs, tortoises, and other animals thriving in habitats around the Tree of Life.

KEEP IN MIND There's a lot you can miss here if you focus only on the park's main attractions. So arrive early and build in time to discover the little gems tucked around the park. If you rush through The Oasis on your way in, plan to see the anteaters, colorful birds, and other Oasis wildlife at day's end. Take Cretaceous Trail in DinoLand to see plants and several critters that have survived since Earth's Cretaceous period. In Harambe, check out the architecture and lifestyle touches (clotheslines on a roof) that mimic real life in coastal Africa.

DISNEY'S WIDE WORLD OF SPORTS

"Take Me Out to the Ball Game," will strike "It's a Small World After All" from your pixie-dusted cerebral playback the instant you spot the old-time baseball stadium at Disney's Wide World of Sports. If it's March, grab those peanuts and Cracker Jacks and settle in to watch home team Atlanta Braves battle the Cincinnati Reds or another National League competitor during annual spring training season. There's hardly a bad seat in the house, and you can explain all about nostalgia to the kids as you take in the sights and sounds of this double-decker stadium and 1950s-style ballpark. From April through September, the Orlando Rays AA minor league team plays a 70-game schedule. So it's one, two, three strikes (who cares), at the old ballgame! After all, it's not whether you win or lose, it's how much fun you're having.

The rest of the year, you may get to see one of 100-plus Amateur Athletic Union sporting events—from field hockey and fencing to table tennis and gymnastics—that take place

KEEP IN MIND Always call ahead or check the Web site for information about spectator events. The NFL Experience and most sporting events are included in the general admission price. You can buy Braves or Rays game tickets at the box office, or check Ticket-Master (tel. 407/839–3900). If you're a Houston Astros or a Kansas City Royals fan, both teams have spring training homes nearby—the Osceola County Stadium in Kissimmee for the Astros (tel. 407/933–2520) or Baseball City Stadium, south of Disney World, for the Royals (tel. 863/424–2500). Check Spring Training under Free Guides at www.flasports.com for other home team locations.

Lake Buena Vista off I-4

 407/363-6600;
www.disneyworldsports.com

 $9.25 ages 10 and up,
$7.25 ages 3-9; Atlanta
Braves tickets $11-$18;
Orlando Rays tickets
$5-$8

10-4 for NFL Experience; professional
and amateur event hours vary

6 and up

in the complex's field house, track and field complex, or on the ball fields. But if you prefer to participate rather than be a spectator, go for the NFL Experience. You and the kids can test your passing accuracy in the Quarterback Challenge, run patterns like NFL wide receivers while trying to catch a ball, and try to kick a game-winning field goal through the uprights while a simulated NFL line charges your way. During other Challenge activities, you can sprint through a football obstacle course, punt, pass, and kick the ball, and check your ball-snapping proficiency. Young children will sprint for the Kids' Zone area, where they can go crazy in the NFL Stadium Moon Bounce and the Balls and Pads playground.

HEY, KIDS! Set your own "sports" record. Have someone time you to see how long it takes to unscramble these words and reveal some of the most popular sporting events: 1) llseabab; 2) oflg; 3) lfobalto; 4) citsmngysa; 5) crecos. Less than two minutes? You're a real pro!

EATS FOR KIDS Hot dog and burger concessions are set up at most event venues, but for a real sports-themed experience, try the **All Star Café** (tel. 407/939-2196; 407/WDW-DINE for priority seating) just steps from the complex. Booths are shaped like baseball gloves, and the place is packed with sports memorabilia and big-screen TV sports action. On the menu: burgers, chicken tenders, and pasta for kids; steaks, ribs, and monster salads for big appetites; plus decadent munchies like chili and cheese fries, Buffalo wings, and potato skins.

First, the kids get their own "passport" to Epcot's World Showcase. Next, they begin a whirlwind tour of the pavilions that represent each international locale. Before you know it, your kids 7 and under are immersed in exploring the cultures of France, Mexico, Norway, China, Germany, Italy, Morocco, the United Kingdom, Canada, Japan, and our own U.S. of A. One key to making Epcot a real adventure for younger children is weaving this "just for kids" passport tour into the agenda. Check into each Kidcot Fun Stop station for a passport stamp and a chance to participate in a craft activity. You can buy the $9.95 passports anywhere in the park, but wait until 1 PM when the Fun Stops open to travel from Future World to the World Showcase.

Meanwhile, head over to the Imagination! Pavilion for a spin on the Journey Into Your Imagination ride. This eight-minute trip, full of special effects and optical illusions, is

EATS FOR KIDS Little ones don't like the wait at many of Epcot's full-service restaurants, so try the Land's **Sunshine Season Food Fair,** with every kid-friendly menu item imaginable in a food-court setting. Or, try the stir-fry and egg rolls at China's **Lotus Blossom Café** or the yummy skewered chicken yakitori at Japan's **Yakitori House.**

HEY, KIDS! Here's your chance to get a head start on the trivia questions posed in the Epcot passport book. What famous desert is in Morocco? What animal represented in the Italy pavilion is the guardian of Venice? What four regions does Epcot's United Kingdom pavilion represent? *Answers: 1) The Sahara. 2) The Lion. 3) England, Scotland, Wales, and Northern Ireland.* Now here's a question that's not in the passport. What famous 20th-century rock band does the British Invasion of the United Kingdom pavilion sound like? *Answer: Why, the Beatles, of course!*

fun for all ages. Little ones also enjoy the Living With The Land boat ride at The Land pavilion. Kids will learn about conservation from animated friends Simba, Timon, and Pumbaa in The Land's 20-minute "The Circle of Life" film. There's plenty at the Wonders of Life pavilion for all ages, including the hands-on Sensory Funhouse. Next door at Universe of Energy, robotic dinosaurs are the main attraction when Bill Nye the Science Guy and several TV personalities lead you on an excursion through time and the history of energy. Once you move on to circumnavigate the World Showcase, let the kids join other youngsters at several Kidcot Fun Stops. Take them on the Maelstrom in Norway—a Viking boat ride past trolls and through hazards of a stormy North Sea. Toward evening, head back to Future World for an "underwater" jaunt past sharks and other sea life in The Living Seas pavilion, or take a slow, steep ride through time and space inside the "big ball" of Spaceship Earth.

KEEP IN MIND As you begin the day, plan some flexibility surrounding the park's kid-oriented activities and entertainment. Don't miss the splash fountains on the walkway between the World Showcase and Future World (pack swimsuits and a towel to share); the British Invasion plus King Arthur and the Holy Grail at the United Kingdom; the huge, colorful model train exhibit at Germany; the Dragon Legend Acrobats at China; the small play area on board a Norwegian longboat between Norway and Mexico; and World Showcase Kidcot Fun Stops.

If a Disney attraction is known for its long lines, odds are it's perfect for kids 8 and older. Honey, I Shrunk the Audience at the Imagination! pavilion in Future World is one of these, so get a FASTPASS appointment (Disney's way of helping you avoid long lines) or arrive first thing in the morning. Based on the movie, *Honey, I Shrunk the Kids,* this 3-D film romp screams with special effects and tactile surprises. If surfing the Internet or playing computer and video games are among your kids' favorite pastimes, trek over to Innoventions East and West. You'll be tempted to stay a while to check out high-tech games and cutting-edge products, so allot time for play and arrange a meeting place and time. Each building is packed with the latest techno-wizardry, from a video game where you can be the action figure to a computer station where you can send a video to friends and family back home. While in Future World, pick up a FASTPASS for Test Track, where a road test ride accelerates to high-speed action. Then hit Body Wars for an exciting simulator journey through the human body at Wonders of Life, and visit Universe of Energy before returning for your Test Track appointment.

EATS FOR KIDS If dining out with kids is now a pleasure, not a chore, Epcot's the place to enjoy it. Best bets are **L'Originale Alfredo di Roma Ristorante** in the Italy pavilion, the **San Angel Inn** in Mexico, and the **Coral Reef,** where an entire wall of the dining room is the Living Seas' monstrous aquarium. Make priority seating arrangements ahead of time at (tel. 407/WDW–DINE); it's always easier to reserve during nonpeak dining hours.

 Lake Buena Vista off I-4

 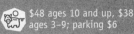 $48 ages 10 and up, $38 ages 3-9; parking $6

 9-9; hours vary in summer and on holidays; Kidcot Fun Stops 1-8

407/824-4321; www.disneyworld.com

3 and up

Home in on entertainment while you're here. The kids can jam to the JAMMiters during a performance at Innoventions, American Vybe at The American Adventure, or MoRockin in Morocco. Kids love the sounds and can even produce their own vibes on sets of drums and bongos at the Outpost between the China and German pavilions. At The American Adventure, complex robotic figures of Ben Franklin and Mark Twain narrate a big-screen musical production of America's story. If the kids are old enough to stay up late, you've got to see Epcot's nighttime extravaganzas. Tapestry of Dreams is a festive pageant with live percussive music and fanciful characters that circles the World Showcase. IllumiNations is a "give-em-all-we've-got" fireworks and laser blowout set to a musical medley—the perfect ending to a day at Epcot.

HEY, KIDS! Most of the Disney "cast members" who work in the World Showcase pavilions are international students working here on a visa. They usually speak excellent English and love to talk with visitors just like you. Spend 10 minutes getting to know some of these students, and you can learn lots about their countries, customs, and family life.

FANTASY OF FLIGHT

41

The great thing about this aviation-themed attraction is that it's not hands-off for kids. When you first click through the Fantasy of Flight turnstile, you walk through the restored fuselage of a Douglas DC-6 before leaning into a cloud simulation to feel the sensation of parachuting to Earth. As you continue the walking tour, the Wright brothers fuel your imagination as you stop to watch old film clips of their first successful flight. Next, it's dark, and you're in the trenches of the Western Front during World War I as a dogfight explodes around you. Touch the wrecked plane next to you. It's okay! Walking into the next scene, you fast-forward to World War II and climb aboard a real B-17 Flying Fortress bomber camouflaged in a "snow-covered" field. Once on deck, you see mannequin gunners and learn about their duties as they drop bombs and shoot down the enemy from 25,000'. As you pass the bomb hold, lean over to see film footage of the bombs exploding below.

After all the historical drama, it's nice to enter the huge, bright hangar that's packed with vintage planes and helicopters, from a replica of the *Wright Flyer* and the *Spirit*

KEEP IN MIND It's easy for families to split up and explore the various planes in the air hangar, but keep a close watch on little ones. The giant seaplane has open windows on its second level for ventilation, and if kids try to hang out the windows, they could take a dangerous fall.

EATS FOR KIDS You can have a tasty breakfast or lunch in the **Compass Rose** 1940s-style diner inside Fantasy of Flight. You'll sit at comfy vintage booths while you hear the aircraft hum in the background. Chili lovers will enjoy the meaty chili, and though there's no kids menu, children will go for the grilled cheese, hot dog, or PB&J served with fries or homemade soup. Breakfast is win-win for everyone, with pancakes, omelets, and French toast among other selections.

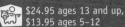

of St. Louis to the Ford Tri-Motor that appeared in *Indiana Jones and the Temple of Doom*. Here, kids can climb into several sectioned cockpits, including a Grumman S-2 Tracker, and fiddle with the controls while playing pilot or navigator. Kids can also explore the gargantuan, two-level Short Sunderland once used for anti-submarine patrol and later converted into the largest passenger seaplane in operation. A door from the hangar leads into Fightertown, where eight simulator-fighter planes sit on the replicated deck of the U.S.S. *Yorktown* aircraft carrier. Once you learn how to keep the simulator steady (ask for a briefing), you'll have a virtual blast shooting down enemy aircraft. In good weather, there's a daily aerial demonstration. The pilot, who often is Fantasy of Flight founder Kermit Weeks, will talk about the plane's history and answer your questions.

HEY, KIDS! Before you take the controls of your fighter simulator, think about what it must be like to take off or land on an aircraft carrier like the *Yorktown*. Planes take off after being catapulted 300' across the ship's deck, racing 0–165 mph in two seconds. To land, planes traveling at about 150 mph make a complete stop on the ship after catching their tail hooks on one of four steel cables stretched across the deck. Experienced flight crews can launch two fighters and land one about every 40 seconds in daylight.

FLEA WORLD

If you've spent enough time and cash in theme-park worlds, point the car toward bargain world, a.k.a. Flea World. There are acres of inexpensive knickknacks for kids to sort through at America's largest flea market (all under one roof, that is). You'll be a happy shopper in this maze of merchandise; a happy snacker at this junk-food jamboree. There's something to interest most any child as they sift through endless displays of model cars, dolls, skateboards, compact discs, athletic clothing, sneakers, jewelry, Mickey Mouse T-shirts, and toys, toys, toys. Kids who have an allowance can plan ahead for how much they want to spend, and you can begin teaching them the art of consumerism. Meanwhile, you'll have plenty of diversion at booths hawking Christmas ornaments, wireless phones, moccasins, figurines, rugs, mirrors, and recreational games and equipment. Scattered throughout the place are snack stands with Pennsylvania Dutch funnel cakes, soft-serve ice-cream cones, fries, nuts, beer, and candy. If you're in the market for hot sauce, Flea World has a mind-boggling variety in flavors that include Acid Rain, Kryptonite, Florida Road Kill, and Shark Bite.

HEY, KIDS! Be a savvy consumer. If you're looking for a baseball cap with your home team insignia, check out the options. You'll probably find caps for $6.99, caps for $17.99, and several styles at prices in between. Most caps are 100% cotton, and the least-expensive style probably will be lighter weight. If you're buying it to wear in Florida, go for the cheap model! Flea market operators often will slash a dollar or two off the price tag if you ask (almost always if your family buys more than one item), so don't be timid!

4311 N. Orlando Dr., Sanford; I-4
Exit 50 E to Hwy. 17–92, right one mile

 Free; tickets 25 for $10;
wristbands $12 or $15;
buy rides and minigolf

 Flea World F–Su 9–6; Fun World
Sa–Su 10–7, some seasonally

 407/330–1792;
www.fleaworld.com

2 and up

Once all that bargain hunting (or hot sauce) has revved up your engine, head on over to Fun World for a spin on a go-kart or a head-on bumper-car collision. Several paces from the flea market, Fun World has separate ride areas for younger and older children. Within its Kid's World section, youngsters 90 pounds and under can board the Space Train, Fire Trucks, Helicopters, and Elephants—all garden-variety amusement park rides at 2 tickets apiece. There's also a Ball Crawl and Jungle Climb. Older kids and adults can swoop down the Giant Slide (2 tickets), whip around the Tilt-A-Whirl (3 tickets), or hop aboard a go-kart (6 tickets) or bumper car (2 tickets). A video arcade makes for lots of big-kid fun, and families can play together on Fun World's 18-hole miniature golf course. Three times daily, Flea World has free family entertainment from magic shows to wildlife presentations.

KEEP IN MIND

Kids like to bargain hunt, too, during a flea market visit. If your kids don't get an allowance, give them a budget and teach them to spend wisely. There are lots of bargains here, but not everything is well discounted, so shop carefully.

EATS FOR KIDS The decadent food is part of the fun here, and booths throughout this 104-acre maze offer pizza, subs, hot dogs, gyros, and just about every junk food imaginable. For a more substantial meal after your visit, **Romano's Macaroni Grill** (I-4 Exit 50, tel. 407/333–4547) has a great kids' menu that includes beverages with each meal. There are lots of Italian specialty choices for the entire family—a local favorite is the chicken scallopini.

FLYING TIGERS WARBIRD
RESTORATION MUSEUM

To kids, a vintage military plane is a wondrous thing. To veterans, it's a nostalgia trip. To Tom Reilly, the Central Florida king of warbird restoration, a restored plane is a gem worth showcasing. For a decade and a half, Reilly and his crew have restored vintage military aircraft and showed them off at his Flying Tigers Warbird Restoration Museum. In many cases, working with little more than a pile of scrap metal, Reilly and his team have restored these historic World War II flying machines to perfection. If you have even a remote interest in planes with a past, you can get right down to the real nitty-gritty here.

Even reluctant visitors dragged along by plane-crazy friends or relatives often become warbird fans after taking the engrossing 40-minute tour here. As you walk through the cavernous hangar, you'll see planes in various stages of repair being worked on by more than two-dozen mechanics and artisans. As they attach propellers, work on sheet metal, and hang engines, you'll be able to smell the grease, see the sparks fly, and hear the rat-a-tat-tat of rivet guns. On your tour you'll discover the stories behind the museum's unusual

KEEP IN MIND The tour can be quite noisy, so if you or the kids are sensitive to noise, you might want to bring earplugs. Because you'll be in the thick of the restoration area, you may encounter dirt or grease. Save your new touring duds for another attraction.

HEY, KIDS! Do you know what a Flying Tiger is? It's a WWII P-40 pursuit plane known for the teeth painted on its nose. From 1940 to 1945, the Chinese paid American pilots to fly these planes in dogfights with Japanese planes. Do you know which bomber was called the Flying Fortress? That was the Boeing B-17 bomber, armed with 13 machine guns and nearly 18,000 pounds of bombs. What was the most lethal WWII German fighter? The Focke Wulf FW190 fighter-bomber. One of these rare machines is currently undergoing a $4 million restoration at the museum.

231 N. Hoagland Blvd., Kissimmee, south of I–4 off U.S. 192

 407/933–1942; www.warbirdmuseum.com

 $9 ages 13 and up, $8 ages 8–12

 Daily 9–5:30; closed Thanksgiving and Christmas

 7 and up

and rare aircraft, from the 1943 Stearman PT-17 once flown by former President George Bush to a French-made plane equipped with a telescope used to aid in landing. If kids are over 48" tall, they can even fly an AT6 trainer with the help of a professional pilot. It costs $140 for 15 minutes of glory at adjacent Warbird Adventures, Inc. (tel. 800/386–1593). The no-charge alternative is to climb inside a jet-fighter simulator and play with the cockpit controls or to stroll the tarmac in the northwest corner of the Kissimmee Airport and watch planes fly while you check out 10 more of the 40 restored aircraft on display.

The museum is laid-back and family friendly. Spend as much time as you like checking out the planes and two rooms full of WWI and II memorabilia, including bombs, guns, helmets, uniforms, and flags. A toy box is available for smaller children who want to play before or after the tour. Even the family cats hang out to meet visitors during tour hours.

EATS FOR KIDS There are lots of chain restaurants nearby, but for a real down-home treat, head to **Joanie's Diner** (120 Broadway, tel. 407/933–0519). You can get breakfast every morning until 11 and Joanie's famous burgers or other specials (try the beef tips and rice) until 6 PM. Every Friday Joanie's has a popular fried catfish dinner 4–7. Saturday and Sunday the restaurant closes after lunch. Kids meals are inexpensive and include a beverage.

Ninety years before the Pilgrims landed at Plymouth Rock, Andalusian cattle imported from Spain were already roaming the Florida flatlands thanks to Ponce de Leon and his cohorts. They're still here, chewing on their cud and now serving as local celebrities at Forever Florida, a wilderness adventure that combines a 2½-hour tour of the 1,500-acre working Crescent J. Ranch and nine Florida ecosystems spread among another 3,200 acres of nature preserve. Forever Florida is the quintessential anti-theme park, a place where cows, deer, snakes, alligators, and hawks perform nothing but their natural behaviors at an attraction that's not afraid to make history and science its focus. You can see the ranch and preserve several ways: on a Cracker coach tour aboard an elevated "swamp buggy" that seats several families at a time, aboard a covered wagon pulled by Belgian horses and mules, or on horseback. Coach tours have great views from seats 10' above the ground and are the best bet for families. They set out at 9, noon, and 3. Take the first or last tour, preferably in cooler weather, to improve your odds for wildlife sightings, which could include

EATS FOR KIDS When at the ranch, plan to eat like the ranchers do. **The Cypress Restaurant** is in the Florida Cracker-style welcome center and has a chuck wagon's worth of goodies for everyone, including gator tail bites, fried okra, a terrific barbecue pork sandwich, and even liver and onions. There's plenty to keep the young 'uns happy, including the usual suspects (chicken fingers, hot dogs, burgers) plus a fried catfish sandwich.

gators, sandhill cranes, and, on rare occasions, a Florida panther. A well-versed guide stops frequently along the way to talk about the workings of Crescent J., its Andalusians or "cracker" cattle, and its beautiful white Charolais breeder cattle from France. You'll drive right through cow territory and probably have to stop for a few to pass.

From the ranch, you'll cross into wet and dry prairies, a marsh, a temperate hardwood forest, two cypress swamps, scrubby flatwoods, and longleaf pine flatwoods. At the Bull Creek floodplain, you'll disembark to amble along a 400' boardwalk that loops beneath palms, cypress, and oaks, their trunks decorated with wild orchids, grapevines, and brilliant golden orb spider webs. At tour's end, kids will want to feed the calves and goats at the ranch petting zoo, or circle the riding ring on a pony.

KEEP IN MIND
Forever Florida was created as a memorial to Allen Broussard, the owner's ecologist son who died after a heart transplant. Future plans include a bio-park where Florida wildlife—including red wolves, Florida panthers, black bears, and bobcats—can be seen in their natural habitats.

HEY, KIDS! Bring a pair of binoculars on the tour—they'll help you spot alligators along the ranch's stream. You may also get to zoom in on Eastern bluebirds or a hawk or swallowtail kite. You'll want to inspect the cypress dome, a stand of cypress trees growing in a dome shape—the tallest trees in the middle stand in a pool of water that boosts their growth. Take a close look through the floodplain—it's the third most-diverse ecosystem in the world after the tropical rain forest (#2) and the tropical reef (#1).

FORT CHRISTMAS HISTORICAL
PARK, FORT AND MUSEUM

Begin with a log fort built during the Second Seminole War, then toss in a walking tour of early settlers' crude log homes, a picnic beneath the oaks, and fun on a first-rate playground, and you have a great getaway with the kids at Fort Christmas Historical Park. You can see everything at your own pace on a self-guided tour, but if the children are old enough to appreciate it, call ahead for the day's guided-tour schedule—tours last about 35–40 minutes.

It was Christmas Day 1837, in the midst of the Second Seminole Indian War, when the U.S. Army arrived in east-central Florida to build a supply depot. Dubbed Fort Christmas, the log fortress housed soldiers as well as ammunition and supplies. When the war ended and most Seminoles were relocated to west and south Florida, pioneers moved in to homestead. Fort Christmas, a sugar cane mill, and seven pioneers' homes are re-created on a plot of the park's 25 acres to create an interesting stroll back through time. Kids can't resist exploring the 80-square-foot fort made of pine logs chinked with sand and lime. The

EATS FOR KIDS No matter where your daytripping begins in Central Florida, there's a **Publix** supermarket nearby. Head straight to the deli's sub station and order fresh sandwiches customized to your family's tastes. The prices are right, and you won't find a better sub anywhere nearby.

KEEP IN MIND While you're in east Orlando, you could combine your fort visit with a **Jungle Adventures** tour (see 27). Or, if everyone's into hiking and wildlife, follow the signs from Fort Christmas Road to unpaved Wheeler Road and into **Orlando Wetlands Park** (25155 Wheeler Rd., tel. 407/568–1706), a large-scale, man-made wetland created to treat reclaimed water and provide a wildlife habitat. The 1,650-acre public park is open Jan 21 through Sept 30 and brims with 160 bird species, otters, foxes, deer, turtles, snakes, and alligators. Admission is free, and park brochures detail hiking roads and trails, as well as wildlife species lists.

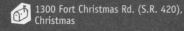

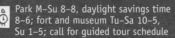

fort's two blockhouses, built as lookouts, are small, air-conditioned museums. One is filled with Native American relics, weapons, and clothing. The other showcases settlers' memorabilia ranging from hand-crocheted pillowcases to old-time toys such as clay marbles. The Pioneer Section of the park gives kids an understanding of just how tough life was back then. Washtubs evoke visions of the women's hard laundry labor, while axes and other crude tools show us that no man's work was ever complete, either. Chamber pots and a wooden outhouse remind us how much we love our modern plumbing.

Set up your picnic beneath the grandfather oaks, and watch the kids get lost in the fun of a playground built like a small fortress or a sandbox complete with child-size digging machines. Older kids might want to bring a basketball or tennis racquets to enjoy the park's courts. They'll hardly have time to eat. If you visit Fort Christmas the first weekend in December, you can watch pioneer demonstrators as they create the goods that were so important to survival in the mid-1800s.

HEY, KIDS! Pioneers had no electricity, so they made their own candles to help light their homes. They also churned their own butter from cream. Children made dolls out of cornhusks, called "corn-shuck dolls." They fanned the husks out at the bottom to make skirts for girl dolls, or tied the husks together to create pants for their boy dolls.

FUN SPOT

Most parents know it's the simplest things that build the biggest fun for kids. Like beating out a tune on pots and pans or making indoor forts out of blankets and coffee tables. At Fun Spot—a mini-amusement park with classic rides and skill games—the simple things rule. There's enough entertainment at Fun Spot to keep several generations occupied and happy for hours on end, from the four go-kart tracks and giant Ferris wheel to the wildly wet Bumper Boats and dizzying, blue-armed Spider ride. Adults who aren't playing Mario Andretti on one of the go-kart tracks can relax on comfy outdoor chairs and even set up a picnic beneath umbrella-shaded tables. And the thrills can seem larger than life, especially for the 8-year-old who drives his first go-kart. Or for the toddler who takes her first twirling teacup spin at the park's Kid Spot (built just for tiny ones) without Mom or Dad riding shotgun.

The outdoor fun is the big entertainment element at Fun Spot. The other is the attraction's indoor Winners Circle Arcade, where welcoming natural light prevents the depressing

EATS FOR KIDS There are plenty of restaurants and fast-food spots nearby, and Fun Spot has its own **Oasis Snack Bar** for pizza and soft pretzels if you can't bear to leave. But for a really unique dinner experience, head south on the tourist drag to **Café Tu Tu Tango** (8625 International Dr., tel. 407/248–2222), where you and your kids can share tapas-size entrees of the Mediterranean variety while watching artists paint and costumed dancers tango down the aisles.

 5551 Del Verde Way, off International Dr.

 407/363-3867

 $30 for 3-hour unlimited use; $3 for one ticket; tokens required for Winners Circle Arcade

Feb–Aug, M–Su 10 AM–12 AM; Sept–Jan, M–Th 2–11 PM, F 2–12, Sa–Su 10 AM–12 AM

 All ages

ambiance of mall arcades. A colorful array of video and other games, played with cups full of tokens, keeps kids happy for hours. The little ones love Wacky Gator, a silly variation on the classic Whack a Mole, the reflex-challenging Spider Stompin', and Ice Ball—a toss-the-ball-for-points game. Older kids and parents can't get enough of Sega racing, skateboarding, and other interactive, high-tech video games. But skip Rapid River by Namco—it's a three-token disappointment. Most of the games spit out tickets for play, and you should plan at least an extra 15 minutes before leaving, for the only painful part of Fun Spot is waiting for kids to redeem their tickets on everything from rings and temporary tattoos to the big kahuna, a 2,500-point giant stuffed Grinch. After shuffling through long lines at many other Orlando attractions, you'll appreciate the bargain prices and practically wait-free rides here.

KEEP IN MIND

Kids have to be at least 8 to drive a go-kart on the easiest track, The Commander. Other tracks have a height limit. But kids who can't or don't want to drive ride free with a paying adult.

HEY, KIDS! Add up the length of the four Fun Spot tracks to figure out how far you'll be able to drive your go-kart: The Quad Helix zips more than 1,600' on four corkscrews and includes a 25-degree banked descending curve; the Conquest spans 1,000' with its "Florida Ski Jump" descent hill; both the Thrasher and the Commander courses are 800' long. That's right—4,200' of track to cover, with or without an older driver depending on your age and height.

GATORLAND

You've got to wonder if the Gatorland animal handler is just a little bit nuts. There he stands in a sandy ring, surrounded by water and several 6' to 8' American alligators. He leans over the water, grabs one of their huge, powerful tails, and begins yanking the chosen one into the ring. After several tries, the handler, or gator wrestler, is astride the toothy beast and insulting the gator's mama as he holds shut the reptile's powerful jaws. "Now be good," he says, "or I'm going to start talking about your mother—she's a handbag in the gift shop." Ba-dum-bum. And so it goes at the Gator Wrestlin' Show, a popular attraction where entertainer-handlers in khaki shirtsleeves and Crocodile Dundee hats do more gator maneuvering than actual wrestling. They hold open its jaw to display 82 really sharp teeth, flip it onto its back before it rights itself, and try to get the audience to mimic a gator grunt. The show is one of several highlights at this walk-on-the-wild-side animal park.

KEEP IN MIND Though you should never feed alligators in the wild, you can feed the Gatorland alligators. Just after you enter the park, buy a packet of cold hot dogs, then watch the feeding frenzy begin as you toss the meat chunks into the water from the park's wooden walkway.

Another Gatorland spectacle, Gator Jumparoo, pits the park's gators against one another as they compete for a whole chicken by leaping skyward to grab a carcass that hangs

HEY, KIDS! 1. How big is a newborn gator? a) 8"–10" or b) More than 2' long. 2. How long can alligators and crocodiles live? a) Up to 30 years or b) More than 70 years. 3. Which has more teeth showing when its jaw is closed? a) Alligator or b) Crocodile. Answers: 1. (a) Newborn gators at 8"–10" fit into an adult's palm. 2. (b) The oldest known crocodile lived to be 77. Some Gatorland alligators are between 40 and 60 years old. 3. (b) Crocodiles show many more teeth than gators when their jaws are closed.

14501 S. Orange Blossom Trail,
Orlando

 $17.93 ages 13 and up,
$8.48 ages 3–12

Daily 9–6 or 7

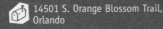 800/393–JAWS;
www.gatorland.com

4 and up

from a line. You can cheer on your favorite contender, and you'll gape unbelievingly as the show's host dangles a chicken between his fingers, daring the gators to jump for it. Beyond the gator shows, there's plenty here for the family to enjoy. Kids can splash around at Lilly's Pad, a small outdoor water-play area with dancing fountains, water jets, and a small jungle gym. The Gatorland Express takes you on a leisurely train ride around the park. And kids love to feed the Petting Zoo goats, llamas, and other critters cones full of chow (watch the cone disappear, too!). Have some fun with snakes and scorpions at an Up Close Encounters show and, before you leave, plunk down $6 for a photo of you holding a python just to prove that Gatorland brings out the nuttiness in everyone.

EATS FOR KIDS Hot dogs, ice-cream cones, and other treats at the snack bar next to the Gator Jumparoo show settle growling tummies. Lunch is on tap at **Pearl's Smokehouse** near the Gator Wrestlin' Stadium where the truly adventurous can sample gator nuggets or smoked gator ribs. If you're looking for fast fare to grab on the way out, **Chick-fil-A** of Southchase Plaza (13085 S. Orange Blossom Tr., tel. 407/251–4612) serves up a tasty chicken sandwich with the usual trimmings.

GREEN MEADOWS FARM

If you give a pig a shoelace, it'll chew it every time. That'll be one of your first down-on-the-farm discoveries when you enter the pigpen and find the friendly little snufflers going straight for your sneakers. At this sprawling animal farm just off the beaten tourist track in Kissimmee, you'll also learn to aim carefully when you milk the cow (or someone may get sprayed); that baby chicks are the cuddliest critters around; and that there's nothing like a picnic beneath the shade of a grandfather oak to help you forget the blitzkrieg pace of theme-park hopping.

The beauty of Green Meadows Farm is in its surroundings and its simplicity. As soon as you buy your tickets, a seasoned farm guide begins the tour, taking you and a small group of other visitors to each animal location. An old-fashioned, tractor-drawn hayride and a spin around the farm on the Green Meadows Express are built into the fun. As you traverse the

KEEP IN MIND When you board the hayride or train, try to grab a seat near the back to avoid the smelly diesel fumes—you'll enjoy the ride a lot more. If little ones aren't sure yet about taking a pony ride, milking a cow, or holding a chicken, don't push them. It's better to let them have their comfort zone and move at their own pace.

40-acre farm, you'll find yourself nose to snout (or beak) with up to 300 critters, including ducks, geese, chickens, pigs, goats, calves, ponies, llama, bison, and, of course, the milking cow. You'll get plenty of time to mix and mingle with the farm animals in each pen, and all the kids have the opportunity to hold or pet the critters as the guide demonstrates how to handle each animal. Watch out for those feisty chickens when you visit the coop; and if your kids do catch one, don't miss the photo op. The pony ride on a small circular track is a thrill for most youngsters.

One of the best times to visit is October, when you can visit the farm's pumpkin patch. Take some pictures, then take home some of these popular pulpy fruits for carving and pie making. It's a great way to celebrate the season.

KID-FRIENDLY EATS Bring your own picnic—a loaf of bread, cheese and fruit, plus some pre-spread PB&Js for the kids. You can buy soft drinks and fruit juices at the farm's concession, but avoid purchasing the microwave sandwiches here unless you're desperate.

HEY, KIDS! Check out how some of the animals are attracted to certain members of your family. Did you notice the way that llama keeps its eye on your dad? This fellow homes in on the tall ones in the group every time. And if you're wearing a shiny belt or shoe buckle, look out for the goats! They love all that glitters. If you slow your pace near the sheep, one may come over and rest her head on your leg. Pat her gently—she thrives on the attention.

GUINNESS WORLD RECORDS EXPERIENCE

33

Setting a world record used to be within the realm of only a fortunate talented few. Now there's a world record for just about everything. A basketball free-throw record (280 baskets in 10 minutes); a most body pierced woman record (290 piercings); and even a Wack-A-Ball record (49 whacks in 15 seconds) by a woman who works for the manufacturer that built the popular arcade game. And you can see it all for yourself at Guinness World Records Experience, an interactive record-fest that's high-tech fun. It begins with a brief, humorous film clip showing how Hugh Beaver of the Guinness Brewery in Ireland founded The Guinness Book of Records in 1951. Next, you can play a hands-on, big-screen version of Guinness World Trivia (simple fun for kids and adults). Afterward, your wacky film host "shrinks" you down to size for entry into the attraction's Computer Gateway and Micro-Technology Playground. Kids love this darkened playground with a super tunnel slide that "feels like being inside a computer," and you'll enjoy more interactive screens featuring video Q&As about medical, animal, and movie records. Everyone will want to take a shot at the Wack-A-Ball and Hoop Skills records here.

EATS FOR KIDS Stay parked and walk to **The Mercado** food court (8445 International Dr.) where food stands provide kid-friendly dining such as chicken tenders at **The All American Grill** (tel. 407/352–8025). Other spots include **Gino's Pizza** (tel. 407/363–3961) and **China Express** (tel. 407/363–1026) for fried rice and other Chinese food standards.

KEEP IN MIND Two things: first, a few records shown here may be frightening to young children—the world's largest tumor (ovarian, 303 pounds) and the most extensive cranial reconstruction (on a boy who was shot in the head). You can pretty much scoot the kids away from these bits of video unless they're very curious, then explain only what they need to know. Second, if the kids love the Motion Simulator Theater—and most do—ask to ride again. The theater has 48 ride seats, and attendants are usually happy to let the family enjoy the experience again. If you get queasy and prefer not to ride with the others, you can grab one of the theater's stationary seats.

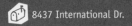

Soon, you're brought "back to size" in the noisy Molecular Expander before stepping into a Space Shuttle simulator that rocks gently back and forth. Here, you can linger and digest lots of space records (the largest sunspot ever recorded was 7 billion square miles!) presented via audio and six video shuttle screens. Finally, it's back to Earth in Guinness Town, a multimedia streetscape where you can ring the doorbell of the world's richest man (Bill Gates, $90 billion plus), check out life-size replicas of the most tattooed and pierced women, and visit a travel agency of world records.

The best is saved for last in the Motion Simulator Theater, where you'll blast off for a record-setting adventure that takes you on a wild ride to the moon and across snowscapes, waterfalls, and railroad tracks. Who knows? You may emerge to set a record as the world's most record-savvy family!

HEY, KIDS! Which animals set the record as best builders—beavers, humans, or termites? Which group of animals has been recorded to weigh the most—a herd of elephants, a swarm of locusts, or a pod of blue whales? And which of these has the most legs—a millipede, centipede, or a Rockettes Christmas special? Answers: 1) termites, recorded to have built a termite mound 42' high. 2) a swarm of 12.5 trillion locusts that flew over Nebraska in 1874. 3) a millipede.

HARRY P. LEU GARDENS

What kid doesn't like to play "detective," even if there's not a real puzzle to solve? The 50 acres of lush landscaping, winding paths, and gurgling streams at Harry P. Leu Gardens provide the ideal setting for a pleasant stroll and some botanical clue gathering for a family game of "plant detective." Bring along a gallon-size plastic bag for each child, and begin your trek in the Ravine Garden. Even though you can't pick flowers or leaves from any of the plants, kids can gather interesting plant or tree material already fallen to the ground for their clue bag, including sweet gum tree seed pods, nutshells, and a variety of leaves. Although there's no real problem to solve, this activity will keep kids focused while you're touring. Back at home kids can create a story to go with their findings, press leaves or flowers, or create a great collage.

As you stroll through the Ravine, keep an eye out for garden snakes that sometimes slither among the colorful bromeliads, banana trees, and elephant ears. Watch butterflies soar

HEY, KIDS! Keep an eye out for these unusual plants while you're at the garden: the resurrection fern with fronds that curl up and appear to die when dry, but expand and flourish with moisture; the three-sided trunk of the triangle palm; and bamboo, which looks like hollow sticks but is actually the largest of the grasses. And did you know that caterpillars thrive on milkweed to become butterflies and that firecracker plants are a hummingbird favorite?

through the garden and light on the orange-flowered butterfly weed. Then it's onward to the Palms, Cycads, and Bamboo section, where you can eyeball a fragrant cinnamon tree (bend a leaf to sniff the spiciness), a stand of bamboo, the ancient Chinese ginkgo biloba tree, and a sago palm, which has been on the Earth since dinosaur days. Other gardens include the rocky, cactus-filled Arid Garden, the Wildflower Garden, the Rose Garden, and a Floral Clock inspired by one in Scotland.

Kids 9 and up are ready for the ½-hour guided tour of the Leu House Museum, where the history of the property's owners comes alive from the days of Indians and log cabins through 1961. The home is filled with antiques and memorabilia of the colorful people who lived here, including farmers, a county sheriff, and an aspiring silent screen actress.

KEEP IN MIND
Since you're on your own in the gardens, you may want to stop for a briefing by a Leu Gardens staffer before you venture out. He or she can fill you in on what to look for and provide some fun facts about some of the plants.

EATS FOR KIDS No picnics are allowed here, but you can find fun eats a few miles north on U.S. 17-92. The steak burgers and shakes are yummy at **Steak 'N Shake** (tel. 407/645-4452). For a decadent treat, visit the **Krispy Kreme** doughnut shop, also north on 17-92 (tel. 407/671-7944).

HOOP-DEE-DOO MUSICAL REVUE

There's a whole lotta foot stompin' goin' on at Fort Wilderness Resort in Walt Disney World, where the Hoop-Dee-Doo Musical Revue has played to packed audiences for almost three decades. This western-style vaudeville show at Pioneer Hall is goofy, sweet, high-energy dinner theater packed with music, dancing, and enough corn-pone humor for the whole family to chew on together. Speaking of corn, you'll get it off the cob at the family-style feast served between acts. Just as you dig into the first course, the show's six Pioneer Hall Players crash onto the stage singing their lively theme song, "Hoop Dee Doo." A ditzy blond dancer with an infectious giggle named Claire; a red-headed Annie Oakley cutup named Dolly; and a bowl-hatted, half-wit punster named Six Bits keep the laughs and slapstick rolling throughout the evening. "You remind me of a cigar-store Indian—you both have wooden heads," Dolly says to Six Bits. His reply: "It's better than a cedar chest!" Some of the players perform a terrific medley of "Shenandoah," "Red River Valley," and "This Land

KEEP IN MIND You'll need a reservation for the trail rides (tel. 407/WDW–PLAY), which leave several times daily from the Tri-Circle-D Ranch and cost $32 per rider. Kids must be 9 years old and at least 48" tall to ride. Buy tickets ahead of time to guarantee seats on the post-show wagon ride.

EATS FOR KIDS Most kids love the Hoop-Dee-Doo grub, which begins with a family-style bowl of dinner salad and loaves of fresh-baked bread served with honey butter and progresses through buckets of fried chicken and tender ribs, corn, and baked beans before the grand strawberry shortcake finale. The dinner includes all-you-can-drink soft drinks, tea, coffee, or milk—and sangria and beer for adults. If you have a picky eater, ask your server when placing your beverage order to bring on some mac 'n' cheese and substitute ice cream or a brownie for the fruity dessert.

is Your Land." The audience gets in on the act by waving cloth napkins during one number and playing metal washboards with spoons during the show's finale. The big show-stopper comes when several audience members, including a child, are picked at random to don costumes and take parts onstage in a hysterical takeoff of "Clementine."

Book ahead for a 5 or 7:15 Hoop-Dee-Doo reservation, then arrive earlier for other Fort Wilderness fun. Take a trail ride or rent a boat for a spin on Bay Lake. Kids can pet goats, pigs, and other critters at the Tri-Circle-D Petting Farm, open most days until 5. After the show, at 7 or 9:30, you can hop onto a horse-drawn wagon ($6 ages 10 and up, $4 ages 3–9) for an excursion through the woods. Time it right, and you'll get to watch the Magic Kingdom fireworks when your wagon pauses by Bay Lake. Who needs the crowds on Main Street, U.S.A. when Mother Nature provides a perfect view from the wilderness?

HEY, KIDS! You'll get a stitch in your side laughing at the antics of Six Bits dressed in a bear skin for the show's "Ballad of Davy Crockett" number. If you can "bear" it, try some Hoop-Dee-Doo-style word play on your friends. Tell them the heat in Florida is a **bear**—so un**bear**able, in fact, that your **bare skin** was the only outfit needed. Nevertheless, you can **bare**ly remem**bear** when you had so much fun! Oh yeah, and don't forget the one about the musical **bear** at Country **Bear** Jamboree who sang tenor, or was it **bear**itone?

HORSE WORLD

First, tell your kids about the cowboys and ranchers who settled the vast Kissimmee cattle country throughout the 1800s. Remind them of the Seminole Indians who hunted the land long before they were forced to live on reservations. Then, climb aboard a regal Andalusian named Fire or a feisty Thoroughbred called Jack and ride into whatever bygone day your imagination can conjure as you hit the nature trails of the 750-acre Horse World riding stables.

Horse World trail guides will match you and your kids with horses of fitting temperaments, and you'll begin your 50-minute riding adventure by rounding the corral where the horses reside. Before you can say, "Hi yo, Silver!" you and your trusty steed are ambling along a sandy trail in the Kissimmee woods. Even a 6-year-old will be riding high and guiding a Horse World mount after receiving simple instructions from a seasoned guide. The music of the woods surrounds you as you pass patches of palmetto and stands of ancient oaks

KEEP IN MIND If you want to encounter more Florida wildlife, such as deer and wild boar, reserve ahead to go on the first ride of the morning in January or February. The colder weather means local critters may be out and about in greater numbers.

3705 S. Poinciana Blvd., Kissimmee

 407/847-4343

 $32 ages 6 and up,
$14.95 ages 5 and under
riding double with adult

Daily 9–5

6 and up

dripping with Spanish moss. Crickets chirp. Birds warble. And an occasional horse's whinny breaks the solitude. Along the way, keep an eye out for butterflies, box turtles, snakes, and even spiders spinning their intricate handiwork.

Riders who've been there and done that should sign up for the Intermediate Trail Ride, which combines a one-hour walk and trot through the woods. It's recommended for anyone older than 9 with some riding experience. Advanced riders should grab for the gusto—an Advanced Private Trail walk-trot-canter ride lasting up to one and a half hours. Horse World has 34 horses in all, plus a few old dogs and some goats that hang out by the stables. If you can make it on a Saturday, the Children's Horse Camp, 9–noon, opens up the world of horses to kids who want to learn about riding, horse care, and safety.

HEY, KIDS! See if you can ride up close to the guide—the younger you are the closer you can probably get. Most of the guides have lots of experience and can give you great tips on handling your horse and spotting wildlife.

EATS FOR KIDS Numerous fast-food outlets line U.S. 192 just before your turnoff onto Poinciana Boulevard. If you want to prolong your stay in the quiet countryside, grab some sandwiches before you arrive and have a picnic on the redwood tables just outside Horse World's gift shop and check-in area.

INTERNATIONAL TROLLEY & TRAIN MUSEUM

There's something fascinating and romantic about trains that captures the imaginations of young children and often endures through adulthood. The International Trolley & Train Museum, though small, displays an enchantingly detailed train setup touted as one of the country's largest operating indoor G-gauge layouts. You and the kids can spend as much time as you like watching the 14 continuously operating trains and three trolleys, and you can even join in a scavenger hunt prepared by museum staff. The 20 challenges on the hunt, which can take 1–2 hours depending on your children's interest in trains, include finding the Abominable Snowman, determining the number of covered bridges, locating the name of the lost elephant, and counting the number of depots. Kids get caught up in the detective work, and adults who are film and television buffs make some fun discoveries along the way. For example, check out the replica of the Munster family's haunted house halfway up one of the display's mountains. There's also the home from *My Three Sons* and

KEEP IN MIND When children see the working helicopter sitting outside the museum, they'll beg to climb aboard. **Helicopter Tours** (8990 International Dr., tel. 407/354–1400) will take three passengers on rides, from a brief $20-per-person, 20-minute local tour to a much more expensive several-hour excursion.

EATS FOR KIDS Breakfast buffs can eat eggs and bacon, pancakes or waffles, anytime at **Denny's** (9880 International Dr., tel. 407/248–1177). **Tony Roma's Famous for Ribs** (8550 International Dr., tel. 407/248–0094) has special perks with its $2.99–$4.99 kids' meals—drink, dessert, and a raw veggies with ranch dip appetizer are part of the deal. The menu is crammed with great bites for adults, too, such as the eatery's "famous" baby back ribs and the onion ring loaf.

8990-A International Dr.

407/363-9002;
www.trolleyandtrainmuseum.com

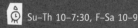
$8.95 ages 13 and up,
$6.95 ages 3–12

Su–Th 10–7:30, F–Sa 10–9

18 months and up

the town hall from the hit film *Back to the Future*. All the while, passenger trains, freight trains, and trolleys are tooting, passing, and climbing more than 2,200' of track that winds around 12' snow-capped mountains. The layout incorporates more than 2½ tons of authentic, used railroad ties from the Florida Central Railroad system, which are built into the mountains for a realistic effect. Small children can grab one of the museum's many plastic step stools for a great view of the layout's farm area, city area, and coal-mining town plus all the tunnels, 8' waterfalls, and more than two dozen bridges positioned throughout the display.

An outdoor ride around the museum on a train pulled by the gleaming red, gold, and silver *Lady Liberty* steam locomotive is a delightful grand finale. Kids who can't get enough can grab a seat every 20 minutes when the train repeats its brief journey.

HEY, KIDS! The major urban center on the train layout is Garden City. When you look around you can see that the city's economy depends on logging, coal mining, manufacturing, and railroading. Look for all these businesses around the museum. The mountains surrounding Garden City were created from chicken wire and cement, and the waterfalls cycle more than 12,000 gallons of water per hour. Two of the falls feed a 300-square-foot lake, and the smaller falls feeds the display's winding river.

There are two very good reasons to brave this park with children 7 and under: Seuss Landing and Camp Jurassic. From the moment you spot the bright colors and playful, looping design of the Seuss Landing area, the much-loved author's verses from *The Cat in the Hat*, *Green Eggs and Ham*, and other classics will dance in your head. Arrive early and head straight to The Cat in the Hat ride to avoid long lines. Thing 1 and Thing 2 re-create the book's chaos all around you as your "couch" car spins and rolls past a multitude of ride effects. For a memorable photo, be sure the kids try on the Thing 1 and Thing 2 wigs or the Cat hat in the attraction's shop. The One Fish, Two Fish, Red Fish, Blue Fish ride lets kids steer their Seuss fish-mobiles up and down as they circle water spouts and dodge a wet hit by following the rhyme's rules. Seussian characters like Dog-a-lopes, Cowfish, and AquaMop Tops replace the traditional merry-go-round critters at Caro-Seuss-el. After all the twirling and whirling, it's time for a break in the If I Ran the Zoo playground. Children will want to splash in the interactive fountains, comb the maze, and explore play stations to interact with Seussian animals.

HEY, KIDS! If you've heard enough Dr. Seuss stories, you'll find it pretty easy to recognize the crazy, colorful creatures of Caro-Seuss-el. See if you can remember which Seuss tales feature these characters: 1) Cowfish, 2) AquaMop Tops and Twin Camels, 3) Dog-a-lopes and Mulligatawnies, 4) Elephant-birds, and 5) Birthday Katroo. *Answers: 1) McElligot's Pool, 2) One Fish Two Fish Red Fish Blue Fish, 3) If I Ran the Zoo, 4) Horton Hatches the Egg, and 5) Happy Birthday to You.*

In the Jurassic Park area, Camp Jurassic is a playland of volcanic proportion. Children's imaginations run wild among the attraction's lava pits and the amber mine with fossilized insects. You'll find rock formations, slides, net climbers, and caves. At Triceratops Encounter, tykes find it hard to believe that the moving, blinking dinosaur isn't real. It's worth a visit if the line is short. At Jurassic Park Discovery Center, interactive computer screens are popular, and kids like to play along with the "scientist" who's overseeing the hatching of a realistic raptor.

Many of this park's rides are unavailable to children under 48" tall, but play areas like Me Ship, *The Olive,* at Toon Lagoon can keep them happy while grown-ups and big kids take turns seeking out thrills.

EATS FOR KIDS Would you eat it in a box? Would you eat it with a fox? Real Seuss fans can't resist the green eggs and ham at the counter-service **Green Eggs and Ham Café.** It's not food coloring but vegetable extract that makes these eggs glow green. For kids who want to meet characters like Cat in the Hat, **Circus McGurkus Café Stoo-pendous** brings on the Cat and others throughout the day while serving buffeteria-style pizza, spaghetti, and fried chicken. The **Pizza Predattoria** and **The Burger Digs** in Jurassic Park offer quick bites for kids on the move.

ISLANDS OF ADVENTURE
FOR KIDS 8 AND UP

It's great to be 8 (or older) at Islands of Adventure if thrill rides are your thing. Every park area except Seuss Landing offers up high-tech roller coasters or the greatest-of-the-great simulator thrills. Zip to the left of the main entrance and head for Marvel Super Hero Island. Get a Universal Express appointment for The Amazing Adventures of Spider Man, then beeline it to the Incredible Hulk Coaster (54" height requirement). Screaming G-force action plasters you to your seat as you catapult toward weightlessness, two subterranean plunges, and seven rollovers. You'll feel as though you've been catapulted through the night sky aboard the Spider-Man ride's moving simulator vehicles (40" height requirement; kids under 48" must be with an adult), where you're caught in a sophisticated simulated battle between the comic-book hero and his nemeses. Next, get ready to get wet at Dudley Do-Right's Ripsaw Falls flume adventure (44" requirement, kids under 48" must be with a grown-up), Popeye and Bluto's Bilge-Rat Barges white-water raft ride (kids under 48" with adult) at Toon Lagoon, and Jurassic Park River Adventure ride into dinosaur danger (42" requirement

KEEP IN MIND Just because children meet the height requirements of a ride doesn't mean they're ready to rumble. Pay attention to their concerns if they hedge about boarding a ride, and don't drag them on anyway just because you don't want them to miss it. Instead, head for the ride's kid-swap area, where one parent can ride, then return to stay with children while the other parent takes a spin. If your young child is a thrill seeker but doesn't meet the height limit, don't try to sneak him on—the requirement is there for safety reasons.

because of wet, 85′ plunge) at Jurassic Park. After you dry off, head to Dueling Dragons twin coasters (54″ height requirement) in Lost Continent. You're likely to encounter long lines at every thrill attraction, so keep using the Universal Express system to avoid monotonous waits.

The entire family will be immersed in the myth surrounding Poseidon's Fury: Escape from the Lost City at Lost Continent. You'll walk through a mysterious temple, feel the sensation of being sucked into a powerful whirlpool, and get caught in a raging battle between Poseidon ("god" of water) and an ancient demon. Stay out of the first row if you don't want to get splashed.

Even kids who've graduated to stomach-churning coasters may wish for the wacky world of Seuss Landing before day's end because . . . "'I like to be here. Oh, I like it a lot!' said the Cat in the Hat to the fish in the pot . . ."

HEY, KIDS! One of the wildest rides here is Dueling Dragons, twin inverted roller coasters—the Fire Dragon and the Ice Dragon—that race toward several "near-misses" on intertwined tracks. Speeds reach up to 60 mph, and at times you'll be only 12″ from the other coaster cars. The Incredible Hulk Coaster launches your ride with the same thrust as a U.S. Air Force F-16 fighter jet, blasting from 0 to 40 mph in two seconds. Special effects in The Amazing Adventures of Spider Man make you feel a sudden "sensory drop" 400′ into darkness.

JUNGLE ADVENTURES

Kids holler with delight when you pull into the small parking lot of the Jungle Adventures roadside attraction and wildlife sanctuary. That's because Swampy The Giant, an alligator-shaped gift shop, awaits with an irresistible photo op for children who can't wait to climb inside the toothy gator grin. The entrance is pure Florida kitsch, but what lies within is an off-the-beaten-path family adventure loaded with interesting nuggets of information about animals and their habitats. You can meet an endangered Florida panther and learn how its species is being threatened by cars, its habitat's destruction, and pollution. You can also cruise a swamp full of alligators and take a walking tour past black bears, gray wolves, crocodiles, snakes, monkeys, and several peacocks strutting their brilliant colors. Finally, you also have the opportunity to visit a small re-created Native American village and learn about its tools, weapons, and household items.

As you enter the park, you walk onto a wooden bridge spanning the green swampy water of this 20-acre wetland area where dozens of American alligators loll in the water. From

HEY, KIDS! Alligators are very cool characters, but girl gators generally are cooler than their brothers. When a female alligator digs a hole for a nest, her eggs are genderless. The eggs laid in the cooler bottom of the nest become girl gators, and the eggs near the top, which is usually a degree or two warmer, hatch into boy gators. And did you know that these cold-blooded reptiles can hold their breath underwater for more than three hours by slowing their heart rate to nearly one beat per minute?

26205 E. State Rd. 50, Christmas, 17 miles east of Orlando

 $14.50 ages 12 and up, $8.50 ages 3–11

 Daily 9:30–5:30

 407/568–2885; www.jungleadventures.com

 6 and up

the bridge, you can watch the Alligator Feast, scheduled four times daily. A park guide appears on a small covered platform above the water and rings a "dinner bell." Faster than you can say, "Come and get it," the gators swim at light speed toward the bell. If you've never seen a 900-pound alligator leap into the air for morsels of meat, you're in for a show. Afterward, a 10- to 15-minute Jungle Cruise on a 20-passenger float boat puts you in the middle of the alligator-infested swamp. While idling along, your driver explains how alligators nest and tells you about the swamp's largest gator, the 13' Goliath.

Because the attraction is rarely crowded, park guides are casual and speak with groups of visitors in an informal fashion. Your guided tour here will take about 2½ hours, and you're welcome to stay and explore on your own as long as you like.

KEEP IN MIND
Younger children may become impatient during the guided tour, so make sure the kids have a decent attention span. You may want to carry a backpack with a small snack to stave off hunger pangs that could strike along the way.

EATS FOR KIDS As you head back to Orlando on Toll Road 408, take the Alafaya Trail exit and stop by **Baja Burrito Kitchen** (423 N. Alafaya Tr., tel. 407/282–6880) in the Waterford Lakes Shopping Center. Kid-size burritos, quesadillas, and other munchkin meals include a drink for just $2.29. Adult-size meals are substantial and tasty in this order-at-the-counter eatery. The shopping center also has a **Chuck E. Cheese's** (tel. 407/382–7121) pizza paradise for those who can handle the frenetic pace.

KENNEDY SPACE CENTER

If you've ever fantasized about exploring the final frontier, consider this space-travel reality check: first, eating in a weightless environment is more like a game of catch as you try to grab wayward morsels. Sleeping means zipping into a bag and strapping yourself down to keep from floating into fellow crew members. And if you think you know the meaning of a bad-hair day, check out some of these astronaut photos . . .

Those with "the right stuff" not only learn to deal with such inconveniences, they actually schedule time to answer questions about space exploration several times daily during the Astronaut Encounter at Kennedy Space Center Visitor's Complex. Near the space shuttle launch site in Cape Canaveral, the complex is a big day's worth of fun where you can see work in progress on the International Space Station, watch some great IMAX space films, revisit the Apollo 8 and Apollo 11 moon missions, and make a virtual visit to the red planet in Mad Mission to Mars 2025.

KEEP IN MIND
Children 4–12 will enjoy a side trip to the complex's Center for Space Education just past the Rocket Garden. Interactive exhibits here include whisper dishes, which let you broadcast your voice across the room, and the Exploration Station consoles where kids can simulate a rocket launch.

EATS FOR KIDS
Next to the bus tour loading area are several dining options. There's the **Lunch Pad,** with all-American burgers, hot dogs, and barbecue sandwiches. A full-service, '60s-themed diner, **Mila's** has plenty of soup, salad, and sandwich offerings. And the **New Frontier Café** serves southern-style barbecue. If you want to do dinner up big after leaving the complex, head to a local institution—**Dixie Crossroads** (1475 Garden St., Titusville, tel. 321/268–5000), popular for its rock shrimp and other native Florida seafood and its sugar dusted corn fritters. Children's options include clam strips, chicken tenders, and shrimp.

SR 528 east to SR 407 north to SR 405 east

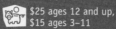 $25 ages 12 and up, $15 ages 3–11

 Daily 9 AM–dusk; closed Christmas and some shuttle launch days

321/449-4444; www.kennedyspacecenter.com

 4 and up

Two live performers play the wacky scientist and his sidekick in the Mad Mission to Mars show, a real giggle-fest for children. Billed as a Mars training mission, the attraction combines audience participation, 3-D film clips, and even a rap version of Newton's laws of motion. Afterward, you line up for a bus to restricted areas such as the International Space Station center where you can actually watch pieces of the station being readied for launch. You'll see the shuttle's huge cargo bay canisters that carry modules into space and return to Earth full of dirty laundry and garbage. It's fun to walk through space-station module re-creations and examine astronaut living quarters. Buses also take you to the complex's Apollo/Saturn V Center for some powerful moon-mission history. Kids are awed by the incredible 36-story-tall Saturn V moon rocket on display. A stop at the LC 39 Observation Gantry gives you a bird's-eye view of the center's twin shuttle launch pads, where space history continues to be recorded with each blastoff.

HEY, KIDS! Since 1950, there have been 3,000 rocket liftoffs from Kennedy Space Center. The Apollo moon missions of the 1960s were completed by the *Saturn 5* rocket, which was nearly twice the size of today's space shuttle, weighed 6 million pounds at liftoff, reached speeds of over 25,000 mph, and had the explosive power of an atomic bomb. Amazingly, the rocket's command module used only 2,000 watts of electricity, the amount typically used by an electric oven. No oven was required for the first meal on the moon— they had packaged bacon "squares," peaches, and sugar cookies.

KISSIMMEE RODEO

The spirit of the American cowboy is alive and kicking in Kissimmee, and that's no bull, pardner. Just gallop on over to the Kissimmee Sports Arena on a Friday night, plunk down a ten spot for a cowboy hat to call your own, and grab a bleacher to watch men, women, and sometimes even children compete in some of the toughest sports around. Riders and ropers, mostly from Florida, serve up plenty of unrehearsed action in the ring with bull riding, calf roping, barrel racing, and team roping sports. Their skills have been passed down by generations of cowboys known as "cow hunters," who had to be skilled in roping and handling cattle that roamed through Florida's swamps and thick palmetto brush.

Your kids 9 and under will be thrilled to learn there's even a rodeo event designed just for them. The calf scramble invites all children 9 and under to enter the ring and race for one of the ribbons tied to several calves' tails. It's fun chaos for everyone in the arena, and

HEY, KIDS! If you're planning to enter the calf scramble, try to line up at the side of the arena near the spectator bleachers. You won't have as far to run when the calves are turned loose, and you may catch a ribbon early. Also, wear boots or old shoes with good soles or tread—sneakers make it hard to maneuver in the dirt or mud. Finally, when the announcer tells you to avoid stepping on any "Girl Scout cookies"—that's rodeo speak for cow patties. Now have fun, y'all!

958 S. Hoagland Blvd., Kissimmee

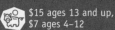 $15 ages 13 and up,
$7 ages 4–12

 F at 8 PM except 3rd F in Feb, 1st F in
Oct, and usually all Dec

 407/933–0020;
www.ksarodeo.com

 5 and up

kids who snare ribbons win prizes from the rodeo announcer. On some nights, several lucky youngsters weighing less than 55 pounds get to try a bareback ride on a sheep in the mutton bustin' event. Most hang on for a second or two, but several have made it past the 5-second mark. It's muddy business once they fall off, but the kids love it.

Traditional rodeo events are exciting for the whole family, and kids like to count the seconds that a cowboy can hang on to his bull or see which cowgirl can race her steed fastest around the barrels. A couple of "rodeo clowns" and an announcer on horseback keep the action lively between events. The Kissimmee Rodeo is an unabashed slice of Americana you can savor one Friday night while everyone else is sweating out a theme-park line.

EATS FOR KIDS

The rodeo concession stand sells hot dogs, boiled peanuts, and other snacks. For some really great grub before the show, head to **Sonny's Real Pit Bar-B-Q** (4220 W. Vine St., tel. 407/847–8888). Tender smoked baby back ribs and sweet iced tea are favorites, and there are lots of other barbecue options, a salad bar, and kid meals.

KEEP IN MIND If the whole family is having such a great time that they don't want to leave after the rodeo action ends, they're invited into the 3,200-square-foot **Catch Pen Saloon.** Here, the rodeo stars, as well as spectators, kick back for a beer and some two-stepping to a live local band. The kids are welcome to enjoy a lemonade and dance until about 11, but the smoke can get thick and uncomfortable if they're not accustomed to it.

LAKE EOLA PARK

"Can we ride the swan boats, please, please?" is the kid chorus heard round the park when families arrive at downtown Orlando's Lake Eola Park. The large, swan-shaped paddle boats, docked near the park's concession in the northwest corner, beckon to all kids fascinated by the idea of pedaling around the lake and hoping to get sprayed by the lake's centerpiece multilevel fountain. Ride first thing in the morning or late in the day when temperatures are cooler—it's a lot of work, and smaller children won't pedal for long before tiring out.

Founded in 1883, Lake Eola Park is the site of many popular events including spring Shakespeare Festival performances in the park's amphitheater, outdoor concerts, arts and crafts shows, and an annual fall festival sponsored by the Disney folks. Its July 4 Picnic in the Park attracts thousands of visitors with family-friendly entertainment, games, and fireworks. But even on a non-event day, Lake Eola Park spells fun. Bring a loaf of bread

KEEP IN MIND Parking is free along Eola Drive, but you'll have to plug a meter if you park on Central or Rosalind. Picnic tables are on the park's east side near the playground, and the grassy expanse here is perfect for kickball or football. Call ahead or ask a park ranger for event information.

EATS FOR KIDS Children love the $1 snow cones at **Champs Lake Eola Café** (tel. 407/839–8899) near the swan boat dock. The Champs concession also serves up cappuccino, sandwiches, and root-beer floats. For a more upscale menu that includes $5 children's meals, stroll to the park's south side and the **Lake Eola Yacht Club** (431 E. Central Blvd., tel. 407/841–0033). **Panera Bread** (227 N. Eola Dr., tel. 407/481–1060) is a local favorite with counter-service soups, sandwiches, and pastries. Outdoor seating is pleasant in spring and fall.

Downtown, bordered by Eola Dr., Central Blvd., Rosalind Ave., and Robinson St.

 Park free; swan boats (3 people maximum) $7.50 per ½ hour

Park open daily 6 AM–12 PM; swan boats available S–Th 10–6, F–Sa 10–8

 407/246-2827

 All ages

and feed the park's families of both black and white swans. Let the kids explore the park's large, mulched playground, where brightly colored swings, slides, and climbers are geared toward toddlers on one side, bigger kids on the other. Stroll the wide, brick-bordered walkway that circles the lake to spot ducks, turtles, fish, egrets, and even anhingas (snake birds) that fish underwater and come up for air revealing only their long, snake-like necks. You might also see anhingas drying their wings on the lake's small southwest island of cypress and palms. Also on the west side is an area fondly dubbed the "Chinese playground" by local school children. Trees trimmed in a bonsai effect surround a small, red wooden bridge, and kids like to hunt lizards on the rocks.

No agenda is required for a visit to Lake Eola. Bring a book, a football, a picnic, a chess board, and—oh, yes—your pedaling shoes!

HEY, KIDS! If you're going to pedal a swan boat, you'd better know how to drive it! These snazzy floating replicas of the park's real swans are steered by a rudder that you turn from the center of the boat. Once you pedal away from the dock, practice steering and turning to get a feel for the boat before venturing across the lake. Try to stay about 20' from the fountain, and start back early if you're pedaling into the breeze when you turn toward the dock.

LEGO IMAGINATION CENTER

Dinosaurs, aliens, and sea serpents, oh my! As you walk through Downtown Disney Marketplace toward the 3,000-square-ft outdoor LEGO Imagination Center, you're greeted by whimsical, life-size LEGO families of aliens and dinosaurs. An enormous, wide-eyed LEGO sea serpent, Brickley, rises above the lagoon sporting a friendly, four-fanged grin. Here, the kid fun is free and parents get to kick back and relax—unless, of course, these brightly colored plastic bricks bring out the kid in you. If you arrive wheeling a stroller, park it by one of the black LEGO parking meters (no charge) in front of the center's 5,500-square-foot retail store.

On the outdoor LEGO playground, imaginations are encouraged to run wild at several themed play stations shaded by umbrella awnings. Under the helpful supervision of two or three play-area specialists, you can build a spaceship or alien invader at the space-themed station, a fortress at the castle-themed station, or a vehicle of your own design at the town-themed station. Your kids can even race their creations on an outdoor racing ramp.

HEY, KIDS! It took 230,000 red, blue, green, yellow, black, white, and brown LEGO and DUPLO bricks to build the family of dino-tourists outside the LEGO Imagination Center. See any resemblance to your own family?

Downtown Disney Marketplace, 1672 East Buena Vista Dr., Lake Buena Vista

 Free

 M–F 9:30–11, Sa–Su 9:30–11:30

 407/828-0065

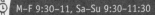 All ages

As your kids enjoy their building odyssey, you'll find it hard to resist plopping down on one of the benches of LEGO red, yellow, blue, and green. Here, you can keep an eye on tots who gravitate toward the DUPLO playhouse—best suited for toddlers or preschoolers because of the bricks' larger size. The playhouse features a small tube slide and building stations designed for tiny hands. At a building board across the play center, six toddler-size tubs of bricks give your wee ones more creative options. Kids are mesmerized by the elaborate revolving LEGO displays of castles, jungles, and other creations in the store's bubble windows that overlook the play area.

OK, so sooner or later you'll wind up inside the store, a virtual cornucopia of building sets, kids clothing, and everything else LEGO. Let the kids spend their allowance—they'll usually make wise choices.

KEEP IN MIND
Be sure to supervise kids in the appropriate play areas. Tots who get burned out on building will want a ride on the Marketplace kiddie train and the carousel ($1 a pop) before you leave.

EATS FOR KIDS Just across the lagoon, you can see the volcano of **Rainforest Café** (tel. 407/827-8500)—the best themed eatery in town—spouting its fiery welcome. You and your kids will love the tasty pastas, ribs, burgers, and dinosaur-shape chicken tenders as well as the jungle ambiance, but try to dine during non-peak hours to avoid the long lines. There's also a **McDonald's** 20 paces from the LEGO playground, or the **Ghirardelli Soda Fountain & Chocolate Shop** for tempting treats.

MAD COW THEATRE

Combine a collection of folk tales with colorful masks, music, and dance, and what have you got? "Cow Tales from the Planet," an entertaining way to introduce theater to children while drawing them into the magic of culturally diverse stories like *Kibungo,* a fable from the Amazon Rain Forest, and *The Boy Who Lived with the Bears,* a North American Iroquois legend. Mad Cow Theatre, an innovative local company performing adult and children's plays since 1997, develops quality children's productions that are shown periodically at one of several Orlando or Winter Park theaters before packing up to tour local schools. Seasonal plays such as *Mole's Homecoming: A Holiday Tail,* based on the classic *Wind in the Willows,* offer something different from the usual holiday fare to mesmerize kids in an intimate theater setting. Audience participation performances like *Purple Cow* blend poetry, rap, rhyme, and rock 'n roll to inspire kids to enter the whimsical world of nonsense verse and maybe even create and perform their own poem.

KEEP IN MIND Call local theaters or Fringe Festival organizers to get a current schedule. If you can organize your visit during the Fringe Festival, you can't go wrong. Make sure to arrive early to get great spots for small viewers since there are no reserved seats.

EATS FOR KIDS A casual spot to dine before a downtown area show is **Anthony's Pizzeria** (100 N. Summerlin Ave., tel. 407/648–0009), where you'll find some of Orlando's best non-chain pizza. Cheese steaks, Greek salads, and other yummy treats help keep everyone in the family happy. If the theater is in the Winter Park area, the kids will love **Taqueria Quetzalcoatl** (350 W. Fairbanks Ave., Winter Park Village, tel. 407/629–4123). You can order your quesadillas, tacos, burritos, and other San Francisco–style Mexican specialties at the counter and enjoy them in a laid-back atmosphere.

 2010 Harrison Ave.

 Call for information

407/297–8788;
www.madcowtheatre.com

 Tickets $5–$15

 5 and up

Mad Cow is just one of several local troupes that produce theater for kids—the Florida Children's Repertory Theatre (SAK Theatre, 398 W. Amelia St., tel. 407/657–4483) is another one of the best. It presents four major productions each year. Interpretations of classics like *Charlotte's Web*, *Peter and the Wolf*, *Rumpelstiltskin*, and *The Emperor's New Clothes* are staged in a small theater and usually involve some level of audience participation. The troupe also participates in the city's annual downtown performance arts extravaganza, Orlando International Fringe Festival (407/648–0077; www.orlandofringe.com). The festival takes place over a 10-day period in late April or early to mid-May, and the Kids Fringe venue (location varies) has a variety of companies performing everything from musical revues to classics to comedy sketches. This massive street fair with face painting, clowns, jugglers, and other entertainers is a great way to show the kids how much fun live theater can be.

HEY, KIDS! See if you can match the main character of each of these popular plays performed by Orlando troupes with the clues provided: 1) Kissed by seven small guys, 2) Needed a fashion advisor, 3) Climbed monster vegetables, 4) Missed the football again, 5) Spun magic for a pig. *Answers: 1) Snow White of* Snow White and the Seven Dwarfs, *2) the Emperor from* The Emperor's New Clothes, *3) Jack from* Jack and the Wonder Beans, *an interpretation of* Jack and the Beanstalk, *4) Charlie Brown, of* You're a Good Man, Charlie Brown, *and 5) the amazing spider, Charlotte, of* Charlotte's Web.

Throughout his life, Walt Disney was a train fanatic. That's why one of the first sounds you may hear as you enter the Magic Kingdom is the perky toot of a 1928 steam engine chugging into the Main Street station. The Walt Disney World Railroad also happens to be one of the few rides in the park you can hop without a wait, and it's a great way to kick off a visit if you're traveling with children 7 and under. Take the train straight to Mickey's Toontown Fair for a whirl on Goofy's Barnstormer kiddie coaster and an audience with The Mouse himself (line up at the Judge's Tent, camera at ready and patience on tap). If the kids liked the Barnstormer and are at least 40" tall, you'll want to make tracks for Frontierland and the Big Thunder Mountain Railroad—a bumpy but kid-friendly coaster with plenty of twists, turns, and drops minus the stomach-churning sensation of a full-fledged roller coaster.

Fantasyland is "kiddie central," and the younger set won't want to miss Peter Pan's Flight, Dumbo the Flying Elephant, and The Many Adventures of Winnie the Pooh. Ditto for

KEEP IN MIND Prices are high inside the kingdom, so cut costs by packing your own water bottles and refilling at fountains, loading your backpack with kid-friendly snacks, bringing your own film and sunscreen, and sharing the meals you purchase. Many kids are more than satisfied with half an individual-size pizza.

Adventureland's The Magic Carpets of Aladdin and the elevated-rail ride on the breezy, line-free Tomorrowland Transit Authority. Hop a raft to Tom Sawyer Island in Frontierland for a break halfway through the day when crankiness sets in and everyone needs a break from the relentless lines. Here, you can take a relaxing walk along shaded paths while the kids explore dark caves, romp across a barrel bridge, and play soldier at Fort Langhorn.

If you haven't seen the 3-o'clock parade, grab a curb early in Frontierland or on Main Street, U.S.A. for a performance. It's a great way to see and photograph all the Disney characters, to hear your favorite film tunes, and to get that contagious pixie-dusted feeling.

HEY, KIDS! Since Walt Disney World opened in 1971, the monorail trains have logged enough miles to circle the moon 30 times!

EATS FOR KIDS A favorite counter-service kid spot is **Cosmic Ray's Starlight Café** in Tomorrowland, where burgers (and veggie burgers), rotisserie chicken, soups, salads, and sandwiches satisfy most cravings. A bonus: the robotic alien Cosmic Ray plays piano tunes as you dine. You'll pay a lot to sup at **Cinderella's Royal Table** (tel. 407/WDW–DINE) in Cinderella Castle, and you'll need to book "priority seating," but it's worth the experience if kids are mature enough to enjoy it.

Children 8 and up will want to drag you straight to Space Mountain in Tomorrowland or Splash Mountain in Frontierland at the beginning of your theme-park journey. If you arrive in the park by the 9 AM "rope drop," the faster you are, the better you'll fare. Or you could use Disney's free FASTPASS option, available at seven Magic Kingdom attractions (check your park map). FASTPASS gives you an appointed time to return, allowing the family to visit lower-demand rides while you wait for "priority" entrance to these park favorites. Remember, you must use one FASTPASS ticket before you can get another.

Of all the Magic Kingdom "lands," Tomorrowland has the most draws for older children. What kid doesn't want to put the pedal to the metal on the Tomorrowland Indy Speedway or orbit colorful planets high above the park, Buck Rogers–style, in Astro Orbiter? Emotional maturity is a must, however, for the ExtraTerrestrial Alien Encounter. This in-the-dark sensory scare-fest has been known to freak out even some adults.

GETTING THERE Disney's famous monorail is a great way to travel from the Magic Kingdom's Ticket and Transportation Center to the park. A tip for the perfect ride: work your way to a waiting area near the front of the train and ask a Disney cast member if you can ride up front with the driver. If another family has already reserved it, ask for the prized seats on the next monorail train. It won't take long, and it's worth it.

If you're traveling with kids of all ages, split up and cover age-appropriate attractions first, then plan to meet for lunch and continue together to explore Buzz Lightyear's Space Ranger Spin and Country Bear Jamboree. Most kids who are not afraid of the dark also clamor for The Haunted Mansion and Pirates of the Caribbean. A few attractions in addition to the Tomorrowland Transit Authority usually keep moving despite crowds, so hit the following while you're waiting for a FASTPASS appointment: Swiss Family Treehouse in Adventureland, a rigorous climb up a winding staircase into this massive tree house fit for a Parade of Homes; and "it's a small world," a whimsical boat tour through many cultures punctuated by the repetitive, unforgettable title song.

Whatever your strategy when you enter the park, be flexible for the kids. If they help develop the game plan, the kingdom will be more magical for all.

HEY, KIDS! The state of Florida doesn't have much in the way of mountains, but two of the highest are right here in the Magic Kingdom: Big Thunder Mountain looms 197' above Frontierland, and Space Mountain is a whopping 180' tall.

MOUNT DORA SCENIC RAILWAY

Your train adventure is off and running the minute you spot the bright red 1931 Pullman coach car that serves as ticket depot for the Mount Dora Scenic Railway. The eye-catching depot is the gateway to a vintage rail excursion through historic Mount Dora and its scenic countryside. Monday through Friday, you can board the Dora Doodlebug, a 1920s-style, 48-passenger Edwards self-propelled gasoline mechanical railway motorcar. The Doodlebug not only has all the bells and whistles that thrill kids (and adults), it's built to drive forward and backward during its eight-mile trek past local landmarks and vast Lake Dora. On the leisurely ride, your conductor talks about the history of this town popular for its antiques shopping and artist community. He'll tell you when you've arrived at Mount Dora's summit (183' above sea level) and point out gopher tortoise burrows by the track. When you hear the train's long whistle followed by a short blast, get ready to cross a bridge high over U.S. 441. Another fun surprise: while stopped on the bridge, you'll stand and flip your seatbacks to face the other direction. Here's where the train reverses direction,

KEEP IN MIND While in Mount Dora, take the kids to Gilbert Park (Liberty Ave. and Tremain). Its huge wooden play gym is well shaded by oaks and designed like a castle with turrets and other fanciful touches. Across the street at Palm Island Park, stroll a nature boardwalk by the lake where raccoons, gators, and other wildlife live. Check out the tiny lighthouse standing sentry over the port—its light guides boaters navigating the lake after dusk. The Mount Dora Chamber of Commerce (341 Alexander St.) near the depot will give you a colorful map and information on boat tours and other diversions.

Alexander St. and 3rd Ave.,
Mount Dora

800/625–4307, 352/383–4368

Dora Doodlebug $10 ages
13 and up, $6 ages 12
and under; Cannonball
train $16 ages 13 and up,
$8 ages 12 and under

Doodlebug departs four times daily
M–F; Cannonball departs twice Sa–Su;
call for schedule

All ages

and the engineer heads to the front of the car where children can take turns peering out the front window at the track stretching before them. After heading back through town and past the depot, you'll continue along the edge of Lake Dora, spotting herons, egrets, and a bald eagle's nest beyond an orange grove. Before the car reverses direction again for its final leg, the conductor gives a brief railroad history, often enlisting the help of youngsters on board.

Weekends, you get a longer ride along a slightly different route in the Mount Dora Cannonball's turn-of-the-19th-century–style coaches powered by an authentic 1913 Baldwin oil-fired steam engine. Dubbed "Florida's Movie Train," it has appeared in feature films that include *Rosewood* and *O Brother, Where Art Thou?* as well as the miniseries *North and South*.

EATS FOR KIDS

At **Snacks 3rd Avenue** (108 E. 3rd Ave., tel. 352/735–1914), boxed lunches with sandwiches, homemade cookies, and ice cream are winners. Kids give the pizza high ratings at **Mount Dora Pizza & Subs** (2718 W. Old U.S. 441, tel. 352/383–5303), and the eggplant parmesan is worth the five-minute drive from downtown.

HEY, KIDS! Federal law requires trains to sound signals alerting motorists and pedestrians of their arrival. Different whistle patterns of long and short blasts signify different warnings. See if you can guess what these blasts mean: 1) long, long, short, long; 2) one long; 3) one short; 4) two short; 5) three short. *Answers: 1) approaching highway grade crossing; 2) approaching station; 3) stopping; 4) proceeding forward; 5) backing up. If your parents let you, you can buy a train whistle at the depot and practice your own train warnings.*

OLD TOWN

If the multicolored lights of the Ferris wheel and roller coaster don't capture the kids within seconds, the carnival aromas of roasting nuts and cotton candy are bound to do the trick. At this festive cross between a boardwalk, county fair, and old western town, your kids will most likely crave an ice cream, beg for a roller-coaster whirl, ambush you in the well-padded Laser Tag attraction, and gaze in awe at those who try out the Human Slingshot. Scattered among a colorful mix of 90-plus rides, shops, and eateries are a Haunted House, a Bungy Trampoline, and even a psychic-reading and hair-wrap joint.

In the Orlando tourist Mecca of highly themed and higher-tech attractions, Old Town is a refreshing step back in time. You queue up to buy ride tickets at booths scattered around the 124,000-square-foot entertainment complex, and off you go to cash them in for Tilt-A-Whirl thrills, Bumper Car battles, and a dizzying romp on the giant boat swing, Pharaoh's

KEEP IN MIND At least five Old Town attractions—Laser Tag, Bumper Cars, Human Slingshot, Haunted House, and Go-Karts—carry extra charges beyond the armband or tickets. Scope them out first before laying down your cash at the ticket booth.

HEY, KIDS! If you want to beat Mom and Dad at Laser Tag, sneak up from behind—they're easier targets that way. It's a cinch finding their hiding places behind the attraction's tent-like walls—just stay low and watch for their feet!

5770 W. Irlo Bronson Memorial Hwy., Kissimmee, one mile east of I-4 on Hwy. 192

407/396–4888

M–F $20 all ages for ride armband; Sa–Su $25; ride tickets 50 cents each; $10 for 22; some attractions extra

Rides M–F 4–11, Sa–Su 12–11; shops and restaurants earlier

2 and up

Fury. Your little ones, ages 2–8, will gravitate toward Kids' Town at the southern end of Old Town, where their own thrills await on Flying Teacups, the Wave Thunder ski boats, the Dragon Wagon coaster, and other rides.

The Old Town street party is even more colorful on Friday and Saturday nights, when classic car owners parade their prize vehicles down the attraction's brick streets, then park them for visitors to admire. Be sure to leave the driving to these car aficionados; the Happy Days Go-Karts attractions is a frenetic field day for Indy-driver-wannabes who break every safety rule on this too-small track. If you can't resist the racing urge, scoot on over to the Happy Days Amusement Center, where you can drive a simulated racer and emerge minus the whiplash.

EATS FOR KIDS Every Wednesday night at **Damon's Clubhouse** (tel. 407/397–9444), in the heart of Old Town, kids under 11 can get their meals of burgers, hot dogs, or chicken tenders served with fries and a drink for a very reasonable 98 cents. The ribs here are fall-off-the-bone tender and seasoned to make you swoon. Other Old Town options are the hoppin' **Cadillac Diner** (tel. 407/397–4004), plus a German eatery and a pizza parlor.

ORANGE COUNTY REGIONAL
HISTORY CENTER

Imagine Florida without Disney, air-conditioning, or interstate highways. Rewind thousands of years to a time when the Sunshine State was the last North American refuge for mastodons and mammoths. Now get set for a journey through time as you meet Florida's Paleo-Indians, witness a Spaniard's first Florida landing, discover how citrus farming and cattle ranching became major Florida industries, and learn when tourism became king. The Orange County Regional History Center lets you explore Florida through the ages via interactive exhibits and film and audio presentations.

At the Orientation Theater, kick back in a rocking chair on a re-created back porch of a Florida Cracker home and hear the crickets chirp while a clever film history of Central Florida unfolds. Kids love The Natural Environment exhibit, with its sinkhole, cave, and endangered Florida manatee displays. The tools, spears, and other weapons Paleo-Indians made with shells and animal bones are a draw in The First Peoples area. A completely restored courtroom in this former Orange County courthouse is a curiosity for judiciary buffs.

EATS FOR KIDS Walk one block west to Orange Avenue and head a few blocks north to **N.Y.P.D. Delicatessen & Brick Oven Pizza** (373 N. Orange Ave., tel. 407/872–6973) for a great pie or sub and a fun time. Celebrity visitors to the restaurant, including the Backstreet Boys, *NSYNC members, and other pop stars, are pictured on the deli's walls. For breakfast or brunch, you can't beat the pancakes or stuffed crepes at **First Watch Restaurant** (63 E. Pine St., tel. 407/841–5544) a few blocks away.

 65 E. Central Blvd.

 407/836-8500

 $7 ages 13 and up, $3.50 ages 3-12

 M–Sa 9–5, Su 11–5; closed Thanksgiving, Dec 24, 25, 31, Jan 1

5 and up

Be sure the kids visit the Cracker cabin of the late 1800s, complete with mosquito netting over the beds, Spanish-moss–stuffed mattresses, and a tiny room where game (squirrels, possums, and armadillos) was preserved in barrels of salt water until it was time to cook it over a log fire for dinner. Seminole Indian village displays are also fascinating, and interactive screens let you visit with today's Seminoles who live on six reservations in southern Florida where they ranch, grow citrus, and run casinos.

In the Tourism exhibit, the "tin can tourist camps" of the early 1900s show the fortitude of travelers bent on the dream of a Florida vacation. Their spirit foretold a trend that would explode into the state's top industry after Walt Disney World opened in 1971.

HEY, KIDS! No one knows for sure why Florida's rural pioneers became known as Florida Crackers, but historians believe the name may have come from the crack produced by ranchers' cow whips or the corn kernels cracked and ground for the food staple known as grits.

KEEP IN MIND Parking is limited to three hours in the lot closest to the history center, so head for the all-day parking garage across from the Orange County Public Library on Central between Magnolia and Rosalind. The history center is one block north on Magnolia.

ORLANDO MUSEUM OF ART

Kids like to draw, paint, and color, yet many parents wonder if their children would appreciate a visit to an art museum. Even if you doubt your kids' interest in something called Art of the Ancient Americas Collection or the African Collection, give the Orlando Museum of Art a try. This cool respite from the area's many noisy attractions is a treasure of permanent and temporary exhibitions that can be enjoyed from a kid's-eye view. How? Begin with the cleverly assembled Gallery Activity Bags that hang on hooks in the gallery hallway. Children are encouraged to spread the contents on the gallery floor and have fun exploring art. Doodle pads, felt boards, texture booklets, and color transparencies are among the bag's contents. A guidebook links the contents with scavenger-hunt–like activities as children seek out paintings and evaluate color, light, brushstrokes, and other elements of the art. One activity urges kids to find Herman Herzog's painting, "The St. John's River Entering the Atlantic Ocean," and view it through the transparencies to determine how the color changes affect the painting's mood. The bag's primary-color

KEEP IN MIND Chat with kids ahead of time about museum rules: keep voices low, don't touch the paintings, and don't run in the galleries. Keep a roll of Life Savers or some other small candy on hand as a reward for appropriate behavior in each museum gallery.

EATS FOR KIDS **Forbidden City Chinese Restaurant** (948 N. Mills Ave., tel. 407/894–5005) is a five-minute drive from the museum. The honey garlic chicken with white rice is popular with kids, and there are lots of other authentic Chinese dishes such as pork and eggplant in garlic, and shrimp and beef in *sa-cha* (seafood) sauce. If the family likes Vietnamese fare, drive a bit farther south to **Little Saigon** (1106 E. Colonial Dr., 407/423–8539) for some of the best in town, including many traditional soup entrées.

 2416 N. Mills Ave.

 $6 ages 12 and up, $3 ages 4-11

Tu-Sa 10-5, Su noon-5; closed M, major holidays

 407/896-4231; www.omart.org

4 and up

paddles are very popular, and children enjoy examining many of the works through each transparent paddle.

In a corner of the museum near the permanent Art of the Ancient Americas Collection is a children's Discovery Center with a touch computer screen, books, and an art table. Here, kids can use stamps and markers to create on paper their own designs similar to those found on the exhibition's artifacts. The collection is filled with fascinating art pieces from more than 30 ancient cultures dating from 2000 BC to the year 1521. Kids can also use the Discovery Center's "Eye Spy" picture boards of animals to try to find similar creatures such as a dog, llama, or frog sculpted, engraved, or painted on the artifacts. The Orlando Museum of Art has many temporary exhibitions along with its permanent displays, which makes it easy to introduce children to the world of gallery art.

HEY, KIDS! There's a lot to discover in an art museum, and the Discovery Center fliers at the entrance to several galleries help make it fun. One flier explains that a portrait is a painting, drawing, print, photograph, or sculpture of a real person. Often, you can guess the feelings (happy, sad, angry) of the people in the portraits of the American Collection. Try it. If an artist were to paint your portrait, what expression would you like to have? What clothing would you wear? Remember, your portrait would say a lot about you.

ORLANDO SCIENCE CENTER

Sparks fly, nature thrives, and mysteries of science unravel as you explore the 12 interactive exhibit halls of the Orlando Science Center. Enter the Power Station, and all it takes is your touch to create sparks via static electricity: your arm's muscle power to crank up a lightbulb. Spend some time at NatureWorks to watch a colony of bees at work, and check out the alligators and turtles cruising the center's re-created swamp. Climb through the yawning maw of BodyZone and explore the interior of a giant model of the human mouth, test your strength and agility at interactive measurement stations in the Measure Me area, and pump some "blood" by turning a lever to simulate how blood courses through arteries. Let the kids become orange farmers in KidsTown, where they pick the faux fruit and run it through a bicycle-driven processor. Other exhibits have their fun with dinosaurs, physics, high technology, the cosmos, lasers and optics, and the entertainment technology of "showbiz science." Vertigo notwithstanding, it's fun to ride the glass elevator that overlooks the swamp habitat and transports you to the exhibit floors.

HEY, KIDS! Get set to play the Circle of Life game during your visit (check map for times and location). Why do polar bears never prey on penguins? What is the largest mammal in the world? Name a male animal that gives birth to babies. Come up with the right answers, and you win stickers, shells, and other goodies. *Answers: 1) Polar bears live at the North Pole, penguins at the South Pole. 2) The blue whale. 3) The sea horse (and its relative, the sea dragon).*

 777 E. Princeton St.

 407/514-2000; www.osc.org

 $9.50 ages 12 and up,
$6.75 ages 3–11;
Cinedome films and
Planetarium shows extra

 June–Aug, M–Th 9–5, F and Sa 9–9,
Su 12–5; Sept–May, closed M

All ages

On Friday or Saturday evenings, take the elevator all the way to the top to star and planet-gaze from the center's silver-domed observatory. Here, kids love the adventure of climbing a narrow spiral staircase for a peek through the largest public refractor telescope in Florida. Or you can scan the skies and catch a glimpse of Saturn's rings and moons from other powerful scopes perched on the observatory balcony.

Don't miss the science center's popular traveling exhibits or the comical Einstein Players, an in-house performance troupe. General admission doesn't include the 310-seat Cinedome's Planetarium shows or its spectacular large-format films, but they're usually worth the extra $4.50 for kids 3–11 and $6 for visitors 12 and up. You feel like you're in the middle of the 8½-story, 8,000-square-foot screen action, whether a volcano erupts, dolphins leap from the sea, or the pyramids of Egypt rise before you.

EATS FOR KIDS

There's a great spot for picnicking just outside in Lock Haven Park, so you may want to bring your own barbecue from nearby **B's Bar-B-Que Diner** (1210 Nebraska Ave., tel. 407/896–6746). The Science Center's 200-seat **OSC Café** offers up kid-friendly fare including pizza and corn dogs, with soups, salads, and daily specials for the grown-ups, but prices are high.

KEEP IN MIND Build in extra visiting time for children 4 and under—they'll want to explore every nook and cranny of KidsTown, where a massive Science Story Tree has stairs for climbing to the top and a fun tunnel inside the tree's gnarled root system. A space-shuttle cabin with sound effects and a two-tiered mini-reservoir for water play are also kid magnets (children can tie on plastic aprons provided for the water experience).

PIRATE'S COVE MINIATURE GOLF

Ever heard the story of Captain William Kidd, the churchgoing businessman who set out to hunt pirates and, before you could say "aargh," became one of the swashbuckling fiends himself? What about Blackbeard, the sword-wielding bandit who plundered his way from the West Indies to Maine in the early 1700s? At Pirate's Cove, not only do you get a fun, first-rate minigolf experience, but you receive a mini-history lesson as well.

Start the little duffers off on the 18-hole Captain Kidd course—it's a simpler course and slightly less expensive, to boot. Look for wooden placards that tell of Kidd's 1696 New York commission to hunt pirates and continue the story at each hole. Hole 5 is a favorite. Here, you enter a cave to tee off as a waterfall crashes against the wall and cracks of simulated thunder resound. Scattered skeletons hint at treachery on the high seas. Meanwhile you discover that Kidd sailed 9,000 miles to the Indian Ocean without capturing a single pirate

HEY, KIDS!
Even if you're tempted to go first, let someone else be the guinea pig. You can learn from their mistakes and have a better shot at each hole.

KEEP IN MIND Unless it's winter, your best time to play is in the evening. If your children are just learning and golfers are lining up behind you, take a break to enjoy the scenery while a few parties play through.

 8501 International Dr.

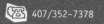 407/352-7378

 Capt. Kidd $7.99 ages 13 and up, $6.99 ages 4–12; Blackbeard $8.49 and $7.49

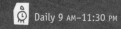 Daily 9 AM–11:30 PM

 5 and up

ship. Children love to linger on the wooden bridge they encounter in front of the waterfall between holes 13 and 14. Several steep downhill holes are inviting—tap the ball gently or it might wind up down the road at Sea World. Kidd's own career went downhill fast when he chose to turn pirate and paid with his life.

The sweet scent of jasmine fills the air and brilliant hibiscus flowers color the landscape as you climb the 18-hole Blackbeard course to its peak, then descend for its final holes. As you negotiate the challenges of hills, rocks, pillars, and rushing streams, share the story of this pistol- and dagger-toting buccaneer whose 18-month reign of terror in the early 1700s ended at Ocracoke, NC, in a surprise attack by the British military. One final warning: beware ye who drive a ball into the drink—'tis a wet path back to the links.

EATS FOR KIDS If you start at 5 or 5:30 pm, you can avoid lines at **Boston Lobster Feast** (tel. 407/248-8606) just south of Pirate's Cove on I–Drive. Any child 11 and under with a whale of an appetite can feast on snow crab, fried shrimp, and more for $14.95, or opt for the $4.95 kids' meal. **Don Pablo's Mexican Kitchen** (tel. 407/354-1345), also a few doors away, is a festive place with lots of kid-friendly eats.

POINTE ORLANDO

Whether it's a Barbie fashion show at FAO Schwarz or a first-run film on the huge screens of Muvico 21 Theaters, there's usually plenty to keep the family entertained at Pointe Orlando—shopping, dining, and entertainment complex. Rows of palm trees line the wide promenades, and several cafés take advantage of the subtropical setting with outdoor dining areas. Jugglers, mimes, and musicians entertain you as you explore the grounds. A popular family stop is XS Orlando, a high-tech playground popular with adolescents and teens who can't resist spending hours riding interactive simulators and playing the latest video games. Radical skateboarding, a virtual Alpine ski race, and video NASCAR racing are just part of the game lineup. Kids also can climb Fun Rock, a two-person, simulated climbing wall that lets you choose your mountain before you ascend.

You never know what themed events (Barbie, Star Wars, and others) to expect at the toy store to beat all toy stores—FAO Schwarz. But one thing is certain. The candy shop just

HEY, KIDS! That 33' Raggedy Ann doll beckoning outside FAO Schwarz gives you an idea of the great toys that await within. Many are classics like Crayola products and LEGO bricks. Here's some toy trivia surrounding three classics. Q. Which of these is not a Crayola color? Macaroni and cheese or Georgia peach? A. *Georgia peach.* Q. How many ways can you put together six LEGO bricks of the same color if each brick has eight studs? 48 ways or 102,981,500 ways? A. *102,981,500.* Q. What's inside an Etch-A-Sketch? Tin beads and plastic gel or plastic beads and aluminum powder? A. *Plastic beads and aluminum powder.*

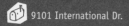 9101 International Dr.

 Free; attraction admissions vary; parking from $2–$5

 Daily 10 AM–11 PM, restaurants and clubs until 2 AM

 407/248–2838; www.pointeorlandofl.com

All ages

inside the store's main entrance is a dazzling "candyland" of tempting confections. Give in to the urge and collect cellophane bags of gummi worms, jelly beans, chocolate turtles, and fudge. Back outside, as you stroll toward the Muvico 21 Theaters, you'll pass dozens of shops—including popular clothing chains and the kid-magnet Disney Worldport shop. Outdoor vendors sell jewelry and souvenirs, including photos of the kids posing with a parrot perched on their shoulders ($9 for a Polaroid). You'll climb a steep staircase to reach the entrance to Muvico 21, where the decor is a dreamy mural of clouds and the deep blue carpet is sprinkled with gold stars. It's one of Orlando's snazziest theaters and a bargain at matinee prices ($5.50 ages 14 and up, $4.50 ages 13 and under). Have a theater employee validate your parking ticket, and you won't mind paying for the popcorn!

KEEP IN MIND XS Orlando (tel. 407/226–8922) opens at daily at 11 and costs $20 for an hour's worth of game play; $25 for two hours. It's best suited for kids 11 and up. Plan to come late morning or afternoon—by night, older teens and a bar crowd predominate.

EATS FOR KIDS Music from the 1950s and 60s plus awesome burgers, shakes, and fries equal plenty of fun at **Johnny Rockets** (Pointe Orlando, tel. 407/903–0762). Chili dogs are gooey but good, and vegetarian burgers are available. Every now and then, servers cut loose and dance to the music for a rousing good time. Adventurous eaters may want to try the mahimahi fingers at **Monty's Conch Harbor** (Pointe Orlando, tel. 407/354–1122). There are plenty of other choices for kids, including grilled cheese and chicken fingers, while grown-ups can dig into conch fritters, and Monty's "famous" fried fish sandwich.

RACE ROCK

Every themed restaurant has its gimmick, and some actually work. Race Rock is a winner in Orlando not just because its turbo-charged racing gimmick is strong, but also because the food is above average, the music is on target, and there's more to do while you're here than just guzzle and nosh. Founded and backed by a hall-of-fame's worth of racers such as Bobby Moore, Jeff Gordon, Richard Petty, Rusty Wallace, and Michael Andretti, Race Rock showcases the motorsport experience in its museum-like exhibits of race-winning NASCARs, hydroplanes, and dragsters, plus the gear and memorabilia of racing legends.

You'll spot Race Rock from I–4 because Big Foot, the world's largest monster truck, is parked outside. It's the perfect photo op for kids clamoring to stand inside its huge wheels. Just outside the enormous circular restaurant, you can ogle Richard Petty's stock car. Inside, more colorful stock cars, dragsters, funny cars, and drag bikes deck the walls and floor

HEY, KIDS!

NASCAR stands for the National Association for Stock Car Racing. Drivers began racing stock cars in the 1930s. The sport evolved from the days when alcohol was illegal and bootleggers dodged police by racing fast cars from their whiskey stills to market their moonshine.

EATS FOR KIDS If your kids have evolved to the stage where their macaroni and cheese doesn't have to be the gooey-from-the-box affair, try the great baked mac 'n cheese with cheddar and Parmesan. It's not on the kids' menu, but they may want to share it with you while munching on the Daytona cheeseburger, chicken dragsters, Grand Prix penne pasta, or other "supercharged" fare. Chicken lovers go for the grilled barbecue chicken gourmet pizza, and there are enough salad, pasta, sandwich, and meat-eaters' items to start everyone's engines. "Racing fuels" that spark smiles are ice cream shakes such as Strawberries and Cream or Chocolate Banana.

 8986 International Dr.

 407/248-9876

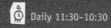 Free; average meal cost
for family of four $50;
game tokens extra

Daily 11:30–10:30

5 and up

and hang from the ceiling. Video screens throughout the restaurant flash clips of racing's great escapes after fiery crashes. You can spend as much time as you like admiring the gear of racing greats, including Mario Andretti and the late Dale Earnhardt. Don't miss the opportunity to talk to kids about racing as a sport for professionals only, not for the driver on the street. Family dinner talk is actually encouraged here by a sound system that keeps rock 'n' roll decibels at a decent level.

Kids can't wait to head straight for the bank of virtual racing games that line the restaurant's lower level. With enough tokens, they can take turns racing hydroplanes, NASCARs, and motorcycles across courses with varying levels of difficulty. Oh yeah, and while you're here, you might as well fill up your stomach with some of the highest-grade themed fuel in town.

KEEP IN MIND You don't have to be a race fan to enjoy Race Rock, but once the kids get a taste, they'll want to sit in the driver's seat. Make it a family affair. Have everyone select their own NASCAR from among the simulated racers—it costs four tokens, or $1 each per race. If the kids are old enough, you may want to continue your racing evening north on I-Drive at Fun Spot Action Park (see #36), where four go-kart tracks put the whole family behind the wheel.

George Van Horn knows his snakes, but he's not immune to their venom. The owner of Reptile World Serpentarium has been bitten by poisonous snakes several times and survived close calls with death to tell about it. At his sprawling house of snakes, Van Horn shares his knowledge of these beguiling reptiles with visitors. Here, you have a snake's-eye view of the deadly green mamba of East Africa, an alarmingly huge Burmese python, and a tangle of squirming rat snakes that would curl the hair of Indiana Jones. Along with a pair of alligators, a pool of turtles, several iguanas, and some talking parrots, 700 venomous and nonpoisonous snakes reside here. Watching the serpents in their glass enclosures is only part of the excitement.

Twice a day, Van Horn collects venom from several species of poisonous snakes, and you and the kids can have a front-row seat for the show in a tiny viewing area. Heck, you can stand right in front of the window that separates Van Horn from visitors as long as the audience is small. Before beginning the dangerous work, Van Horn brings out a nonpoisonous

EATS FOR KIDS A few miles west of the serpentarium on Rte. 192 is a down-home eatery not to be missed—the **Sweet Earth Restaurant** (710 13th St., tel. 407/892–2911). Chicken and dumpling soup and the Philly cheese steaks are stupendous; giant specialty waffles topped with hot fudge or apples and brown sugar melt in your mouth. **The Catfish Place Restaurant of St. Cloud** (2324 13th St., tel. 407/892–5771) is a local favorite for fresh fish.

5705 E. Bronson Memorial Hwy.,
S.R. 192, St. Cloud

 407/892-6905

 $5.50 ages 18 and up,
$4.50 ages 6–17, $3.50
ages 3–5

 T–Su 9–5:30; venom program 12
and 3; closed Labor Day–Oct 1 and
Christmas

 5 and up

Eastern indigo snake for the kids to handle. Next, he disappears through a door and emerges behind a window, where he places a Southern copperhead snake on a table inches from the glass. With help from an assistant, Van Horn nearly immobilizes the snake's head and holds it between two fingers as it bares its fangs, strikes, and pierces the plastic covering of a tall glass. Venom streams into the glass during several strikes. For a half-hour to 40 minutes, Van Horn repeats the collection procedure with some feisty Florida cottonmouths, an enormous Eastern diamondback rattlesnake, and several magnificent monocled cobras. It's high drama with no pretense that will thrill the kids and make your palms sweat. In all, Van Horn collects the venom of 50 snakes a day and supplies it to 400 research labs and universities, as well as to companies that produce life-saving antivenin for snake-bite victims.

KEEP IN MIND
The kids might witness feeding time, when snakes are slowly swallowing mice or turtles and alligators are consuming dead baby chicks (cast-off rooster chicks sold for this purpose). Make sure you explain the reptiles' eating habits ahead of time and prepare children who've never seen an animal eat its natural prey.

HEY, KIDS! Depending on their size, snakes eat everything from bugs and frogs to mice, birds, and even rabbits. Snakes can actually unhinge their lower jaw to fit large prey into their mouths. Venomous snakes use their fangs to put poison in their prey, and even though they don't consider humans to be prey, they can be dangerous if you get too close. If you see a snake and aren't sure if it's venomous, take several steps backward, then run to tell an adult.

RIPLEY'S BELIEVE IT OR NOT!

Step right up, folks, to see a genuine shrunken head, a portrait of the *Mona Lisa* made from 1,426 tiny pieces of toast, and a wax re-creation of the world's tallest man. If it's weird or unusual, you'll find it at Ripley's Believe It or Not! Orlando Odditorium, a 9,000-square-ft gallery that appears to be slipping into one of Florida's infamous sinkholes at its International Drive location. Robert Ripley was an oddity in his own right; a rich, eccentric explorer who traveled the world in search of the bizarre. He published his first best-selling *Believe It or Not* book in 1929 and became famous for his syndicated cartoon series of all things peculiar. It's only fitting that part of his collection of relics—whether twisted, hilarious, or simply amazing—should end up in the Orlando Odditorium.

Kids love this place, especially if they can read well enough to absorb the details on plaques posted near every display. They marvel at the photos of Ubangi women with lip disks the

EATS FOR KIDS Calypso music and tropical treats set the scene for dinner several blocks south on International Dr. at **Bahama Breeze** (8849 International Dr., tel. 407/248–2499). The standard kids menu is jazzed up with exotic fruit coolers and shakes, and inventive appetizers and entrées with a Caribbean twist keep adults happy.

KEEP IN MIND Only a few displays, such as the Medieval Torture Room, can be inappropriate or frightening for children. Make a beeline through those areas to keep nightmares at bay. Near the halfway point of your excursion, a bizarre film showcases illusionists swallowing swords, light bulbs, and even a padlock and key. Skip it, or at least prepare the kids for a gross-out experience. When the padlock and key are regurgitated, keep reminding yourself, "It's only make believe."

size of small Frisbees and laugh at a sideshow of mythical creatures, such as the furry trout from Canada's Lake Superior that was one taxidermist's idea of a fun fish tale. The "Dog-Gone Weird" room, featuring a photo of a Louisiana dog that frequently snatched and wore its master's false teeth, prompts even more giggles. And that's not all, folks. It's hard to get children out of the Tilt Room, which is built on several levels to confuse your eye and your brain with dizzying results. Toss the cue ball onto the pool table and it rolls . . . up! Let the kids romp inside the world's largest tire—it's a great photo op. Turn your senses loose in the equilibrium-altering lava tunnel. And bring along some pennies to uncover the mystery of the Black Hole and its gravitational pull. Now pull yourself together and stumble back to your car. And you will stumble, Believe it or not!

HEY, KIDS! Take a look at some of the ingenious art in the Odditorium—the *Mona Lisa* toast art, the penny portrait of Abe Lincoln, and the family portrait one artist made with lint she collected from her neighbors' clothes dryers. And get a load of that Rolls Royce built from more than one million matchsticks. Now it's your turn. Invent your own art with shells, twigs, or dare we suggest . . . hairballs? If only Ripley were still alive to discover it.

Happily, the focus at SeaWorld Orlando is on the animals, even though thrill rides share space with the park's water-born stars. If you have youngsters 7 and under in tow, there's a way to see these wonderful sea creatures while avoiding large crowds most of the time. Be sure to arrive by the foghorn's opening bellow, pick up a park map, and make a beeline toward the left and Dolphin Cove. It will still be early enough for you to find a spot at the water's edge where you can dangle your arm in the water while you wait for the playful dolphins to swim past. You'll be able to stroke their backs or flippers, if they get close enough, and they usually do. When you're through here, dash next door to the Stingray Lagoon to do the hand-in-the-water thing again. Kids love the "slimy and cool" feel of the rays, and you'll love the wash-up stations with soap and paper towels. Next, circle around to the dolphins' underwater viewing area for a whole new perspective of these intelligent mammals—they love to show off for an audience. Forward march to watch a herd of laid-back manatees, then head straight to Penguin Encounter where these comical

HEY, KIDS! Get ready for the big-screen quiz you'll take while waiting for Shamu to make his grand entrance. Do killer whales have natural predators? How many teeth does a killer whale have? Are killer whales endangered? How much food can Shamu eat each day? Now see if you're ready for the Shamu challenge. *Answers: 1) No. Killer whales are at the top of the food chain. 2) Up to 52 teeth! 3) No. Killer whales are abundant. 4) Shamu can eat up to 200 pounds of food a day.*

flightless marine birds playfully splash and swim, then congregate on rocks for a post-dip social.

One animal show certain to tickle kids' (and your) funny bones is "Clyde & Seamore Take Pirate Island" at the Sea Lion and Otter Stadium, so break up your park tour here. The otters, seals, and walruses are up to some hilarious high jinks in this well-orchestrated performance on a ship set.

Don't forget swimsuits, towels, and water shoes for the kiddie pièce de résistance—Shamu's Happy Harbor. This massive playground combines a large water play area with spots where kids can climb, dig, bounce around, and imitate their favorite water mammal tricks.

KEEP IN MIND Two SeaWorld attractions charge a fee in addition to the admission price—the Sky Tower ($3 per person) and Paddle Boats ($6 per boat). Kids often beg to ride to the top of the Sky Tower, a circular, glassed-in viewing area that revolves as it rises for a gull's-eye view of the park, so be prepared ahead of time with a game plan if you're on a tight budget.

SEAWORLD ORLANDO
FOR KIDS 8 AND UP

Kids 8 and over usually prefer to seek and conquer the park's major thrill rides before settling down for an animal tour. Kraken, a giant roller coaster that sets the Orlando benchmark for height and speed (15 stories, 65 mph), has no floor or sides and gives riders 54" or taller good reason to scream. Be warned that your kids should be coaster-savvy before embarking on this monster. Journey to Atlantis is a milder kind of water coaster right next door that does a good job of getting you soaked during two steep flume plunges.

The entire family should take the journey to Wild Arctic together. You'll be tempted to stay awhile and watch the polar bears, walruses, and beluga whales from behind the glass that encloses their chilly habitats. This attraction's ride is an exciting motion-simulator film trip across frozen tundra that most adventurous kids 42" and taller won't want to miss.

KEEP IN MIND It's not a well-publicized attraction, but families who discover it love the park's Caribbean Tidepool and Tropical Reef. Children can lean above the tidepool and touch crabs and sea urchins, and the Reef's aquariums are filled with starfish, jellyfish, and other fascinating small creatures.

EATS FOR KIDS Pizza and pasta are usually kid pleasers at the park's **Mama Stella's Italian Kitchen** (tel. 407/351–3600 ext. 2), but try to arrive before or after peak dining hours because service is generally very slow. The park has eight other restaurants with options for every palate. The nightly **Aloha Polynesian Luau Dinner and Show** (tel. 800/227–8048) requires reservations. Parents, there's a free treat for you when you stroll over to the Anheuser-Busch Hospitality Center—a complimentary beer.

Small children and the faint-hearted can see the same film minus the motion in a separate theater. Across the lagoon, Terrors of the Deep is a great walk-through aquarium that you can see at your own pace. Crafty moray eels slink out of crevices in the underwater rocks and glide past the glass, often provoking the same oohs and aahs as the exhibit's sharks and barracudas.

The park's big star, Shamu, rocks by day and night for kids of all ages. The Shamu Adventure Show and the nighttime Shamu Rocks America performance at Shamu Stadium show why killer whales are king of the ocean and are among nature's smartest animals. Watch as Shamu's human trainers surf and frolic with the mammoth creatures. And laugh when Shamu drenches the audience—but only if you were smart enough to sit in the second tier.

HEY, KIDS! Try to time your Penguin Encounter for 2 PM. At that time, you can participate in a question-and-answer session with an aviculturist (penguin expert) working inside the icy exhibit. One lucky guest gets to go behind the scenes and touch a real South Pole penguin. Or talk Mom and Dad into a guided tour with a SeaWorld education specialist ($7.95 ages 10 and older, $6.95 ages 3–9; book at the park's entrance)—you may get to see rescued animals being rehabilitated or even touch a shark or penguin.

SPLENDID CHINA

9

In 1974 a Chinese farmer digging a well in Shaanxi Province unearthed a splendid discovery—broken terra-cotta soldiers and bronze weapons buried with an emperor some 2,000 years earlier. The archaeological dig that followed revealed an army of 8,000 life-size statues of soldiers, horses, fighting vehicles, and treasure that dead Emperor Qin Shihuangdi believed would accompany him on his journey to the hereafter. At Splendid China, a 76-acre theme park partly owned by the Chinese government, you can step through a cavelike opening into a re-creation of the tomb with statues one-third the size of those discovered. You also can marvel at a half-mile reproduction of the Great Wall (made of 6 million tiny bricks) as it dips and curves across the park landscape, explore a ¼-scale replica of the Stone Forest in Yunnan Province shaped by centuries of wind and rain, and watch Chinese performances of music, folk dance, and martial arts.

If kids are curious about other cultures, they'll become absorbed in the park's 60 landmark miniatures. There's the Imperial Palace on a terraced incline, a water village of southern

EATS FOR KIDS On U.S. 192 near the park entrance are a **Denny's** (7631 W. Irlo Bronson Hwy., tel. 407/396–0757), **Shoney's** (7640 W. Irlo Bronson Hwy., tel. 407/397–2779), and **I-Hop** (6065 W. Irlo Bronson Hwy., tel. 407/396–0406), where you can fill up on a big protein and carb breakfast to prep for your excursion. In the park, avoid the bland and pricey fast food at **The Seven Flavors** cafeteria. The park's **Suzhou Pearl Restaurant** has an impressive menu of authentic Chinese dishes and is worth a visit.

3000 Splendid China Blvd., Kissimmee

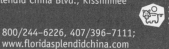 $28.88 ages 13 and up,
$18.18 ages 5–12

 Daily 9:30–7; evening show 6

800/244–6226, 407/396–7111;
www.floridasplendidchina.com

 7 and up

China with doorways that open to the waterway, and the Flying Rainbow Pagoda said to give off rainbows when sunlight strikes the building's glaze. At most replica sites, a push-button audio presentation gives a brief description of each display's history, and hundreds (sometimes thousands) of tiny ceramic figurines represent the people of that time. Some exhibits, including a 30' Leshan Grand Buddha, are the original size. If younger children get restless during the tour, let them unwind in the kiddie play area. Splendid China's elaborate four-act evening show is included in park admission. The live stage spectacle at the 750-seat Golden Peacock Theatre changes its name and theme periodically but always has a cast of talented acrobats, dancers, martial artists, and musicians. It's worth returning for if you leave the premises earlier in the day, but don't forget your receipt for return admission.

HEY, KIDS! If you think the park's Great Wall of China looks long, consider this: the real wall is more than 4,000 miles long and between 15' and 30' thick. The wall first began to go up around 700 BC when farmers wanted to protect their property from raiders.

KEEP IN MIND You won't want to visit when the temperature rises above 85 degrees. There's a lot of walking involved (about 3 miles) and not enough shade. Your best strategy is to fuel up on a big breakfast, then arrive when the park first opens. Guided tours cost extra ($5.35 each for the walking tour, $48.15 for a cart that carries five) but help aid understanding of the history behind many landmarks. The Potala Palace site in the park represents the Dalai Lama's home before he was forced into exile in 1959. Because of the political controversy surrounding this, there are often small groups of protesters at the entrance gates.

TITANIC THE EXHIBITION

Though you won't be in over your head at *Titanic* the Exhibition, you'll still understand the sinking feeling experienced by passengers and crew when their ship hit an iceberg in this immersion into one of the world's greatest sea disasters. At one point in the tour, you're led to a room with a wall of ice. Here, you learn how and why the *Titanic* sank that fateful night in 1912. Then you're invited to press your hands against the ice for 15 seconds. You feel the unbearable cold that blanketed doomed travelers and the ship's survivors, and it gives new meaning to a "hands-on" interactive experience.

The one-hour tour of this museum-like exhibition is led by actors in period costume and blends history and entertainment from the moment you receive your admission, or passage, through your "debarkation." Your ticket bears the name of a passenger or crew member who sailed on the *Titanic,* the largest and most luxurious sailing vessel of her time. Your

KEEP IN MIND Younger kids may find it hard to understand some of the guides' accents. There's a lot of reading involved on the tour if you want to soak up the details—help children understand the event's historical impact by reviewing the display placards with them.

HEY, KIDS! The *Titanic* was the largest ship ever built at the time—882½' long, the length of nearly two football fields. The ship carried approximately 2,200 passengers, but only 675 survived. The ship, which sank in the early morning of April 14, 1912, after hitting an iceberg on her very first voyage, now rests 2½ miles—more than 12,000'—on the floor of the North Atlantic Ocean. A French-American expedition discovered the *Titanic* in 1985 and later confirmed that it had split in two before sinking. The bow and stern were found lying 1,970' apart.

8445 International Dr., in the Mercado

 407/248-1166, 877/410-1912; www.titanicshipofdreams.com

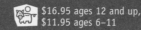 $16.95 ages 12 and up, $11.95 ages 6-11

 Daily 10-9

9 and older

guides lead you through full-scale re-creations of several rooms from the ship, including the grand staircase made famous in the 1997 film *Titanic*. When you enter the chilly "ship's deck," you're surrounded by a clear, starry night sky identical to the one passengers enjoyed before their ship was destroyed. Several hundred artifacts and treasures are on display, including dishes, a life preserver, and letters from passengers. The actor-guides, often with British accents, tell stories like that of the passenger whose suitcase never made it on board—he was the only survivor to retrieve his luggage. When the guided tour ends, you can stay as long as you like to revisit the displays and pore over the pictures, artifacts, and movie memorabilia tied to this tragedy. Visit the memorial wall to learn the fate of the traveler whose name is on your ticket. Though your chances of holding a survivor aren't great, maybe you'll beat the odds.

EATS FOR KIDS There are plenty of eateries close by, and **Damon's The Place For Ribs** (8445 International Dr., tel. 407/352-5984) is a short stroll away in The Mercado shopping and entertainment center. Damon's has a kids' menu that offers all the standards and a favorite of young seafood lovers—shrimp. **Charlie's Lobster House** (tel. 407/352-6929), also in The Mercado, has fish-and-chips and fried shrimp on the kids' menu, as well as burgers and chicken strips. The Mercado food court serves up less-expensive alternatives for the whole family.

TYPHOON LAGOON

Little kids crave the adventures of big kids, but they also want to feel safe. At Typhoon Lagoon, there's a comfort level for younger children at many of the park's wet attractions that lets them be big kids for a day. Central Florida's prettiest water park, Typhoon Lagoon is thick with tropical greenery and built to make you feel like you've been stranded on an island of fun. Sandy beaches surround the lagoon itself—a wave pool surging with almost 3 million gallons of water. The park's "volcano" centerpiece, Mt. Mayday, is topped by the shrimp boat, "Miss Tilly," which supposedly landed there during a typhoon. Kids get a kick out of the geysers that shoot skyward from the mountaintop, and they have a great view as they splash in the lagoon's shallows. They'll also want to conquer their very own watery paradise, Ketchakiddie Creek. Built for children under 4' tall, Ketchakiddie Creek keeps them happy with small water slides, a grotto with waterfalls, sprinklers, and squirting whales. Grown-ups can relax by the pool's edge as the tykes play. Older siblings can take on the park's thrill adventures—including the Humunga Kowabunga speed slide, the Storm Slides that snake through caves and tunnels, and three white-water raft rides.

HEY, KIDS! When Disney Imagineers (the creative team) designed Typhoon Lagoon, they invented a whopper of a story to go with it. The legend goes that a major storm struck the deluxe Placid Palms Resort, turning it upside-down and inside-out, and leaving Miss Tilly stuck on top of Mt. Mayday. Four-foot waves rolled across the lagoon, and tropical fish swam in the lagoon's Shark Reef. Instead of crying over the wreckage, the resort's residents proclaimed their topsy-turvy paradise to be the "world's ultimate water park." Judge for yourself!

Lake Buena Vista off I–4

 $29.95 ages 10 and up, $24 ages 3–9

 Daily 10–6; hours may vary seasonally

 407/824-4321; www.disneyworld.com

1 and up

The whole family will enjoy an inner-tube ride along Castaway Creek, a 3'-deep waterway that circles the park and passes through cool caves and grottos. The tubes are large enough to accommodate adults with a small child if the kids aren't ready to float along on their own. The beauty of this ride is that you can get off at several stops along the way, returning later to complete the 2,100' course.

Now let's review. You aren't really in Central Florida. You're in a hammock beneath a palm on a tropical island, and you're happy. The big kids are going for the thrills. The little kids couldn't be more pleased with themselves. Hakuna Matata! No worries.

EATS FOR KIDS

Your best bet is to bring a cooler with your own picnic (no glass containers allowed). Tables are set up at Castaway Cove and Get-away Glen. Quick food options are burgers, hot dogs, and pizza at the park's **Leaning Palms** eatery and **Typhoon Tilly's Snack Shack.**

KEEP IN MIND Beat the crowds by arriving early and settling your gear in a choice location. Show little ones how to hail a lifeguard or other Disney cast member if they get lost—you'll be reunited with them at High and Dry Towels. Rent a locker to store any valuables ($4 or $6 plus a $2 deposit). You can get free life vests if needed. Typhoon Lagoon closes for about one month each fall for refurbishment; but Disney's other two water parks, Blizzard Beach and River Country, are open at that time.

To keep tots happy in a theme park, it helps to have lots of interactive play. At Universal Studios, Woody Woodpecker's Kidzone achieves that goal without boring adults and big kids. Children 7 and under simply are crazy for this attraction's Curious George Goes to Town area—especially the Ball Factory where you can collect your own arsenal of foam balls and blast them at friends, family, and unsuspecting visitors. The entire playground recalls the mischievous monkey's high jinks, and kids can climb through cages, yank levers, and spray water. Fievel's Playland gives kids a mouse's-eye view in a play area of oversized cowboy boots, cattle skulls, and other props from the film *Fievel Goes West*. Woody Woodpecker's Nuthouse Coaster is a quick, tummy-tickling spin mild enough for tots. Tykes over 36" can ride with a grown-up, kids 48" can ride alone.

KEEP IN MIND It makes sense for the grown-ups to split up, one with the younger set and another with the older kids, so everyone can have a great time without being forced to wait outside age-inappropriate attractions. Regroup for shows, the Nick tour, and meals.

Although Universal is known for its teen appeal and the movie-themed thrills it delivers, A Day in the Park with Barney will lure the littlest ones with its musical show and playground. If you're happy and you know it, you'll exit the film and special-effects show singing

EATS FOR KIDS **Mel's Drive-In** in the park's Hollywood area is a hit with its burgers, fries, shakes, and '50s music. At **International Food & Film Festival** near *Back to the Future . . . The Ride*, you get the convenience of a food court—like eatery and lots of kid-friendly choices including pizza, pastas, Southern fried chicken, and dessert bar. **Classic Monsters Café** in Production Central has monster salads, more pizza and pasta, and vegetarian selections. Frankenstein and other monster celebs make the rounds. If it's your birthday, visit **Café La Bamba Mexican** in Hollywood at 3:30 PM. Each day, they cut a cake for celebrants.

Barney's "I Love You" along with the wee ones. At *ET* Adventure, you ride the bike with ET himself across the night sky—it's magical even if kids haven't seen Steven Spielberg's classic film. The FUNtastic World of Hanna-Barbera (40" height requirement) lets little ones in on a cartoon-filled, motion-based ride minus the turbulence of most simulators. Yogi Bear foils Dick Dastardly to save Elroy Jetson in this wild and wacky escapade. Then, head to the slime geyser to begin your Nickelodeon Studios Tour. You'll pass through the Nick kitchen to learn how gak and slime are made, and you'll test new Nick games in the Game Lab. For the tour's happy ending, one "lucky" kid gets slimed.

KEEP IN MIND Actually meeting the cartoon characters at Universal Studios is a hit-or-miss proposition—Yogi, Shrek, Rugrats, and others appear unscheduled in different areas of the park. Keep a lookout for Scooby Doo and Shaggy when they wheel around the studios in their Mystery Van.

Kids 8 and up will have a field day here as they hop from wild rides to movie-themed scare-fests. Use the Universal Express system, which allows you to reserve a window of time at each attraction, one at a time, to avoid long waits. At *Men in Black* Alien Attack (42" height requirement), you'll feel like you're in a giant ride-through video game as you fire alien-zapper lasers at targets. Prepare for out-of-control spins when the aliens shoot back. If you dig out-of-control weather you'll love *Twister* . . . Ride It Out. Hang onto your hats and remember—it's only special effects—when you hear the freight-train roar of this five-story twister and feel the winds and rain generated by high-speed fans and tanks of water. Special effects also give you King Kong's banana breath in Kongfrontation and a monster shark with an attitude in *Jaws*. Both are rides that begin innocently enough and culminate in the revenge of menacing movie villains. The cyborg villains of the "Terminator" films are frightening enough at the cineplex, but they're even scarier in 3-D at *Terminator 2:*

EATS FOR KIDS CityWalk, Universal's nighttime dining and shopping complex just outside the park, has a lineup of fun restaurants that can all be contacted at tel. 407/224–3663. Older kids will get a thrill out of having dinner at **Hard Rock Café** where the music is loud and the fare is big burgers and other themed-eatery standards. At **NBA City** you can get a great barbecue chicken pizza and shoot some hoops. **NASCAR Café** is popular for its steaks, burgers, and video racing simulators. And if you really want to enjoy that cheese-burger in paradise, it's **Jimmy Buffett's Margaritaville** for some laid-back munching.

 1000 Universal Studios Plaza

 800/407-4275, 407/363-8000;
www.universalorlando.com

$48 ages 10 and up,
$39 ages 3–9

Daily 9–6; closing hours vary
seasonally

3 and up

3-D. This futuristic robot romp stars the usual film suspects—Arnold Schwarzenegger and Linda Hamilton in 3-D—as well as real stunt performers who interact with the audience. Then it's *Back to the Future . . . The Ride* (40" height requirement) with Doc Brown, the absent-minded professor of the film series. You'll ride in his DeLorean simulator for a really hair-raising adventure back in time. At the Hitchcock show, expect a plot twist similar to those in the famous director's films. If you have to miss anything, skip Earthquake: The Big One.

The whole family will want to see the Wild, Wild, Wild West Stunt Show, an action-comedy show with a behind-the-scenes look at how movie stunts are performed. After tangling with a nasty shark, surviving a "Twister," and warding off aliens, a little cowboy humor goes a long way.

KEEP IN MIND
If you're visiting in October and you love Halloween, don't miss the park's infamous "Halloween Horror Nights." Teens especially love the monster madness that attracts big crowds with state-of-the-art haunted houses, convincingly made-up ghouls and monsters, and the "Festival of the Dead" parade.

HEY, KIDS! *Twister . . .* **Ride It Out** has the world's largest indoor tornado vortex, created by dozens of high-speed, 7' fans and with rain generated by 1,500 gallons of water per show. *Men In Black* **Alien Attack** has the largest robotic theme-park creature built—a 30' alien with 8' teeth and 20' claws. The shark in *Jaws* is a three-ton terror almost as scary as the 30' wall of flames shooting from the water during your boat ride. James Cameron, who created the Terminator movies, helped direct **Terminator 2: 3-D,** which is shown on 23'-high, 50'-wide screens.

WEKIWA SPRINGS STATE PARK

15

When you splash and swim in the Wekiwa Springs or canoe down the Wekiva River, it's not hard to imagine the land 2,000 years ago when Timucuan Indians speared fish or stalked deer in the uplands. The clear, cold Wekiwa Springs were named for the Creek Indian word meaning "spring of water." These are the headwaters for the Wekiva River, also Creek for "flowing water." The state park pays tribute to its 2,000-year-old Native American history in the tiny museum near the park's concession.

As you push your four-passenger canoe from the small, sandy beach into the Wekiva River, you'll glide onto an open waterway that soon narrows and flows beneath a drape of oak leaves and Spanish moss. You can paddle with the current of the river, or head upwater into Rock Springs Run when the river forks. You'll spot lots of turtles swimming and sunning, and often you'll see otters playing in one spot while an alligator basks on a log downstream.

EATS FOR KIDS To fill your picnic basket, try **Petty's Meat Market** (2141 S.R. 434, Longwood, tel. 407/862–0400). For dinner, kids love the **Roadhouse Grill** (2300 W. S.R. 434, tel. 407/682–5065), where they can shell peanuts while waiting for a kids' meal. On Tuesday, children eat free.

KEEP IN MIND When you stop at the Ranger Station to pay the park entry fee, ask for a copy of "A Self-Guided Walking Tour" created by students of the Clay Springs Elementary School. This terrific guide takes you on a 900-yard walk through part of the park and keeps children busy looking for a sinkhole, a hammock, wildlife, and air plants such as resurrection ferns. Animal track prints help them determine if an endangered Southern black bear, a deer, or a bobcat might have passed by recently.

Dragonflies flit past, and silvery webs glitter among the oak branches. Lift your paddles into the canoe and float silently to hear the music of crickets punctuated by the splash of a fish or turtle. Children 5 and older usually last up to two hours—there's so much to watch for along the way, and they like to take a brief turn at paddling.

Go canoeing early, then take a dip in the jade-colored Wekiwa Springs in the heat of the day when the 72°F crystal water feels refreshing rather than chilling. Forty-two million gallons of water a day flow through the main spring where visitors swim, snorkel, and float on rafts. Watch the kids closely—no lifeguards are on duty. Afterward, set up a picnic, then head out on a hike or let your little ones scramble around the playground.

HEY, KIDS! Florida is known for its sinkholes, which at times have swallowed the cars and homes of area residents. They form when water erodes the underground limestone and creates a pocket of water beneath the soil. During dry conditions, the soil collapses to form a sinkhole. The one by the Wekiwa Springs is about 15' deep and filled with plants including palmettos, sweet gum, and wild grapes. Don't walk in it, but keep an eye out for animals such as snakes, raccoons, and opossums.

WEST ORANGE TRAIL

4

There's no place like a long and winding scenic trail to venture out for some family fun. Though there are other great trails in Central Florida, the fully paved West Orange Trail has it all, including a place to rent bicycles of all frames (toddler seats available), skates, and helmets. A snazzy, full-color map details every rest stop from the County Line Station's Mile Marker 0 and continuing along the latest extension past Mile 19 in Apopka. And, there are playgrounds and picnic spots at Miles 5 and 7. The 14'-wide paved surface is open to walkers, joggers, hikers, bikers, skaters, and even horseback riders—more than 50,000 people traverse portions of the trail each month. So strap on your helmets, fill water bottles, and review the map's rules of the road with kids before heading out on your adventure. Make sure they understand that they must stop at every stop sign to watch for traffic. Kids under 12 should be warned to wait for the family before crossing.

If children can ride without training wheels, they usually have the stamina to complete a 14-mile round trip. You should begin at County Line Station and plan several hours for a

HEY, KIDS! If you're riding round-trip from Mile Marker 0 to Chapin Station's Mile 7 and back, traveling at 7 mph and taking two 10-minute rest stops, how long will the trip be? Got it? OK, now try this: if you can't get enough pedaling and travel 24 miles round trip at 8 mph, stopping for a 15-minute ice-cream break at Downtown Brown's, a 15-minute playground break at Chapin Station, and two five-minute restroom breaks, how long will your trip take? *Answers: The first trip is two hours and 20 minutes. The second trip is three hours and 40 minutes.*

17914 State Rd. 438, Winter Garden

 Bike rentals $5 first hour, $4 second, $3 additional hours; skates $6, $5, and $4

 Trail, sunrise to sunset; Bikes & Blades, days and hours vary seasonally, call ahead

407/654–1108, Bikes & Blades rentals 407/877–0600, 888/281–3341

 18 months and up

leisurely tour. You'll cross a restored railroad bridge and, before you've gone 2 miles, discover the 110-acre Oakland Nature Preserve that borders gigantic Lake Apopka. The peaceful buzz of crickets and the calls of area bobwhites are common background music on your ride, and you can watch all species of butterflies dance in the butterfly garden at the Tildenville Outpost near Mile 3. You also can stop at the Winter Garden Heritage Museum (open 1–5 daily) to see railroad memorabilia and Native American artifacts near Mile 5. There's a playground here for the 5-and-under set, and a bigger playground with a jungle gym for all kids at Mile 7's Chapin Station. This is a good place to stop, rest, and play before turning around to pedal or skate to the finish.

KEEP IN MIND
Florida law requires riders under 16 to wear a helmet. Carrying a cell phone for emergencies is a good idea. You should also bring sunscreen, sunglasses to help cut glare, and snacks to fortify riders. Build in break times for small children so they don't become grumpy and tired.

EATS FOR KIDS Several good restaurants are along the trail in downtown Winter Garden. **Restaurant a la Mexicana** (2 E. Plant St., tel. 407/654–1998) serves up authentic tacos, enchiladas, and other Mexican treats, as well as chicken nuggets for the pickiest of palates. **Choctaw Willy's of Winter Garden** (99 W. Plant St., tel. 407/905–9917) is a local favorite for barbecue, especially the smoked turkey and ribs. **Downtown Brown's** (126 W. Plant St., tel. 407/877–2722) is a deli that rules kids with its malts, shakes, and 24 flavors of ice cream.

WET 'N WILD

onsider the names of some popular attractions at Wet 'n Wild—The Storm, Black Hole, Mach 5, and The Surge—and you'll know why this water park is a favorite among adolescents and teens. These slides are the ultimate draw for kids craving a slippery slope to wedgie world or a spiral drop through tunnels and flumes. A relentless pop beat blares from park speakers to complete the "scene" for kids and adults who just want to have fun.

If you're hitting the park in the morning, arrive early and grab lounge chairs by the park's 17,000-square-foot centerpiece, Surf Lagoon. Mark your base camp with beach towels, then head off for some family fun on The Surge, a multipassenger tube ride that snakes down five stories of banked curves before plunging into a pool. Another family tube ride is the Bubba Tub, but this six-story, triple-dip slide crosses over into "thrill" territory. It's not for the chicken-hearted, who may want instead to ease into the Lazy River for a leisurely

HEY, KIDS!

You and your siblings or friends can orchestrate a simultaneous splashdown on Mach 5, which has three flumes dumping into the same pool. Just tell the attendant you want to synchronize your slide, then get your blue float mats ready, and go!

EATS FOR KIDS A picnic makes sense if you're planning to stay here awhile, but you can't bring alcoholic beverages or glass containers. Beer is sold in the park, along with a variety of counter-service soft drinks and munchies such as burgers, salads, smoked chicken, and pizza. If you want to make a big day of it, grab lunch or dinner at **McDonald's** (6875 Sand Lake Rd., tel. 407/351–2185), billed as "The World's Largest McDonald's." This two-story fast-food wonderland has the requisite climbing and play area, plus an arcade, a pizza station, and a Mickey D's Ice Cream Parlor with shakes, sundaes, and splits.

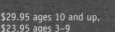

tube trip along a gentle stream. Daring souls, however, will push on to The Storm. Here, you body coast solo at high speeds after dropping from a chute into a giant open bowl where you spin to a splash landing. The Black Hole is a two-passenger tube ride that shoves off into a dark, twisting and turning close encounter with aliens. Whew! And those are merely a few drops in the Wet 'n Wild thrill bucket.

It's not all for big kids. Good swimmers as young as 5 enjoy some of the thrill slides, and they also have a blast climbing ropes to the top of Bubble Up and sliding down the wet, beach-ball–like surface. Toddlers have it made at Kids' Park, with its huge, shallow pool, mini tube slides, anchored water guns, and rope swing. And for the really big kids, like Mom and Dad? Well, if they're not up to a Knee Ski around the park's half-mile lake, the Surf Lagoon will do just fine.

KEEP IN MIND If you're visiting in the heat of the summer, late afternoon or early evening can be an ideal time to show up at Wet 'n Wild. You'll avoid getting scorched, and you'll get a $10 discount off admission after 5 PM. The park's open until 10 most summer nights, so it's a great deal. No matter what time of day you visit, plan to rent a small locker ($5, plus $2 deposit) where you can stash valuables while you swim. Beach towel rentals are $2 (plus $2 deposit), but life vests are free.

WINTER PARK AND SCENIC BOAT TOUR

The charm of Winter Park beckons the minute you spot the first large blue road sign imploring that you "Please Drive With Extraordinary Care." Home of Rollins College, one of the finest private liberal arts colleges in the country, Winter Park is an old-money town with contemporary appeal that offers a kid-friendly respite. First stop: the Scenic Boat Tour, a fascinating, hour-long cruise along the historic city's chain of lakes and canals. Aboard an 18-passenger pontoon boat captained by a local skipper, you and your family will first cruise the 158-acre Lake Osceola, named for the famous Seminole chief who once led a tribe of more than 5,000 Native Americans. Kids love the ride on an open boat, and your skipper keeps things interesting with his narration of local lore and details about flora and fauna.

Before the ride is over, you'll glide along two other lakes and two narrow canals bordered by age-old cypress trees, regal palms and pines, and massive oaks. In the early part of the 20th century, the canals were hand dug so that loggers could float trees to a nearby sawmill.

EATS FOR KIDS Tony Park Avenue restaurants are not exactly geared toward children, but **The Briarpatch** (252 N. Park Ave., tel. 407/628–8651) has plenty of fun eats for kids, from a PB&J sandwich to spaghetti or chicken fingers, and it's a great soup and sandwich spot. **William J. Sweet's Ice Cream & Yogurt** (122 E. Morse Blvd., tel. 407/647–6961) is a fine place to put a sweet finishing touch on your Winter Park getaway.

East Morse Blvd. off Interlachen, Lake Osceola

$7 ages 12 and up, $3 ages 2–11

Daily 10–4, boats leave on the hour; closed Christmas

407/644–4056

5 and up

You may see a rat snake gliding along the canal wall, an alligator basking on a homeowner's beach, or a snowy egret perched near the water. Several American bald eagles live in one of the pine trees and are often seen perched or soaring above Lake Osceola. Opulent mansions and estates along the way include a home where Franklin D. Roosevelt once spent the night and where Harry Truman received an honorary degree.

After you disembark, let the kids burn up some energy a few blocks away in Central Park where there's lots of room to run or play hide-and-seek behind old oak trees. Try to wait for a train to pass by the Amtrak station that borders the park's west side. Few children can resist the spectacle of a freight engine ripping past with its string of multicolored cars or a silver passenger train snaking to a stop at the station.

KEEP IN MIND
If you want to stretch your visit, drive west on Morse Blvd. to Rte. 17–92 and take a right until you reach Winter Park Village. A movie theater with stadium seating, a Border's book store, and several shops and popular restaurants are great choices for topping off the day.

HEY, KIDS! As you cruise the Winter Park lakes, watch for large birds sitting on logs or boat docks with their wings spread wide. They're called anhingas, and they can dive underwater to fish because they have no oil on their feathers. Indians called them "snakebirds" because, when they come up for air while fishing, their long, flexible necks look like snakes rising from the water. When the fishing is done, they sit in the sun to dry their wings.

WONDERWORKS

You know you're in for something different as soon as you spot the WonderWorks upside-down mansion. The story goes that the "teetering" lab blew in from the Bermuda Triangle when a scientist's tornado-making experiment went awry. Now you can tackle your own experiments inside this hands-on, entertainment-rich, three-story interactive science playground. Bolster your balance and walk through the (seemingly spinning) Inversion Tunnel into a world of natural Earth phenomena. Sit through an earthquake measuring 5.3 on the Richter scale, and hang on in the Hurricane Hole as high winds blow in. Watch water drip toward the ceiling in the Antigravity Chamber, then take the interactive Famous Disasters quiz. (And, by the way, note that mosquitoes have 47 teeth and that one second equals one billion nanoseconds.) Kid-friendly science trivia plaques are posted throughout WonderWorks.

Ratchet up the fun further on the second floor, where you ride a virtual glider above the Grand Canyon, wave hoops of giant bubbles through the air, measure the speed of your

KEEP IN MIND
In addition to LazerWorks, the third floor is filled with token-for-play arcade games. Four tokens are $1, 20 for $5, and 45 for $10. To keep costs down, stay on the first and second floors as long as you can before departure time.

EATS FOR KIDS
WonderWorks has its own snack bar with pizza, hot dogs, smoothies, and soft-serve ice cream. For something more substantive, walk across the parking garage to Pointe Orlando, and grab a table at **Dan Marino's Town Tavern** (9101 International Dr., tel. 407/363–1013). Kids can have soup, salad, or fries with their PB&J or one of several other entrees ($2.50–$4.95) while you nosh on sesame seared tuna or filet mignon.

 9067 International Dr.

 407/351-8800;
www.wonderworksonline.com

 $15.95 ages 13 and up,
$11.95 ages 4–12; lazer
tag and arcade extra

 Daily 9 AM–12 PM

 4 and up

fastball, play a keyboard with your feet, climb a vertical rock wall, and try to find perfect balance on a shaky platform (hint: bend over a bit at the waist). You also can design a wild roller coaster on a computer and then ride your creation in one of two 2-passenger simulators—spirals, barrel rolls, corkscrews, and all. (And, by the way, what bodily function can reach the breakneck speed of 200 mph? The sneeze!) Kids like to hang for a while in the Strike A Pose room, where they can transfer their dance gyrations to colorful shadows and designs on a big screen. You'll enjoy the interactive How Old Are You Really? Quiz that assigns you a "health age" based on eating, exercise, and other habits.

LazerWorks on the third floor is one of the world's largest laser tag attractions, accommodating 25 people for each 7½–minute laser shoot-'em-up session. If you've got $5.95 apiece ($3.95 for each extra session), it's fast-paced fun for the entire family.

HEY, KIDS! Here's your chance to play Stump the Grown-ups. Try out these WonderWorks trivia questions on them: How many hearts does an octopus have? What percentage of the Earth's water is drinkable? What is the largest organ in the human body? What sense is most closely linked to memory? Where are a cricket's ears? How hot is lightning? *Answers: 1) Eight. 2) Only 1%. 3) Skin. 4) Smell. 5) On its knees. 6) Lightning can reach 50,000 °F, five times hotter than the sun's surface. Ouch!*

CLASSIC GAMES

"I SEE SOMETHING YOU DON'T SEE AND IT IS BLUE." Stuck for a way to get your youngsters to settle down in a museum? Sit them down on a bench in the middle of a room and play this vintage favorite. The leader gives just one clue—the color—and everybody guesses away.

"I'M GOING TO THE GROCERY..." The first player begins, "I'm going to the grocery and I'm going to buy... " and finishes the sentence with the name of an object, found in grocery stores, that begins with the letter "A." The second player repeats what the first player has said, and adds the name of another item that starts with "B." The third player repeats everything that has been said so far and adds something that begins with "C" and so on through the alphabet. Anyone who skips or misremembers an item is out (or decide up front that you'll give hints to all who need 'em). You can modify the theme depending on where you're going that day, as "I'm going to X and I'm going to see..."

FAMILY ARK Noah had his ark—here's your chance to build your own. It's easy: Just start naming animals and work your way through the alphabet, from antelope to zebra.

NOT THE GOOFY GAME Have one child name a category. (Some ideas: first names, last names, animals, countries, friends, feelings, foods, hot or cold things, clothing.) Then take turns naming things that fall into that category. You're out if you name something that doesn't belong in the category—or if you can't think of another item to name. When only one person remains, start again. Choose categories depending on where you're going or where you've been—historic topics if you've seen a historic sight, animal topics before or after the zoo, upside-down things if you've been to the circus, and so on. Make the game harder by choosing category items in A-B-C order.

DRUTHERS How do your kids really feel about things? Just ask. "Would you rather eat worms or hamburgers? Hamburgers or candy?" Choose serious and silly topics—and have fun!

BUILD A STORY "Once upon a time there lived..." Finish the sentence and ask the rest of your family, one at a time, to add another sentence or two. Bring a tape recorder along to record the narrative—and you can enjoy your creation again and again.

GOOD TIMES GALORE

WIGGLE & GIGGLE Give your kids a chance to stick out their tongues at you. Start by making a face, then have the next person imitate you and add a gesture of his own—snapping fingers, winking, clapping, sneezing, or the like. The next person mimics the first two and adds a third gesture, and so on.

JUNIOR OPERA During a designated period of time, have your kids sing everything they want to say.

THE QUIET GAME Need a good giggle—or a moment of calm to figure out your route? The driver sets a time limit and everybody must be silent. The last person to make a sound wins.

HIGH FIVES

TOP FIVE
Magic Kingdom
Islands of Adventure
WonderWorks
Mount Dora Scenic Railway
Hoop-Dee-Doo Musical Revue

BEST OUTDOORS
Wekiwa Springs State Park

BEST CULTURAL ACTIVITY
Cirque du Soleil

BEST MUSEUM
Fantasy of Flight

WACKIEST
Guinness World Records Experience

NEW & NOTEWORTHY
Florida Audubon Center for Birds of Prey

SOMETHING FOR EVERYONE

ALL AROUND TOWN

Green Meadows Farm **34**
Horse World **30**
Kissimmee Rodeo **25**
Old Town **19**
Splendid China **9**

LAKE WALES
Bok Tower Gardens **54**

MAITLAND
Audubon's Center for Birds of Prey **57**

MOUNT DORA
Mount Dora Scenic Railway **20**

ORANGE CITY
Blue Spring State Park **56**

ORLANDO
Harry P. Leu Gardens **32**
Mad Cow Theatre **22**
Orlando Museum of Art **17**

POLK CITY
Fantasy of Flight **41**

SANFORD (NORTH)
Flea World **40**

SANFORD/NORTHEAST OF ORLANDO
Central Florida Zoo **51**

ST. CLOUD
Reptile World Serpentarium **12**

ST. CLOUD AND HOLOPAW
Forever Florida **38**

TAMPA
Busch Gardens **53**

TITUSVILLE AREA
Canaveral National Seashore **52**

MANY THANKS

Loving thanks to my husband, Walter Benjamin, my sons, Nathan and Sam, my parents, Jack and Charlotte Hess, and in-laws and friends, Jean and Helen Benjamin, for being willing, insightful assistants in the quest to research Orlando's many fun stops. Thanks to Pam Brandon and Michael Cooney for their great advice and research, and to friends Debbie Beckman and Jay and Evan Boyar for lending support with this project. Thank you, also, to Larry White, Lake Eola Charter School parents and teachers, and many other fun-loving folks who offered ideas and assistance.

Finally, this book is so much better thanks to Melissa Klurman, my Fodor's editor, whose keen eye and insights kept me on track at all times.

— Jennie Hess

the end.